THE UNDERDOG

How I Survived the World's

Most Outlandish Competitions

VILLARD (V) NEW YORK

THE JOSHUA DAVIS
UNDERDOG

Published in the United States by Villard Books, an imprint
of The Random House Publishing Group, a division of Random
House, Inc., New York.

VILLARD and "V" CIRCLED Design are registered trademarks
of Random House, Inc.

ISBN 0-345-47658-1

Printed in the United States of America on acid-free paper

www.villard.com

9 8 7 6 5 4 3 2

Book design by Simon M. Sullivan

FOR TARA

We improve ourselves
by victories over ourself.
There must be contests,
and you must win.

—EDWARD GIBBON

CONTENTS

IPSKI-PIPSKI
AND ME

When I visited my dad in Los Angeles as a child, he would sit on the edge of my bed and tell me stories as I fell asleep. These weren't like the stories my mom read me every night back home in San Francisco. Dad liked spy thrillers, but at age five I didn't understand much. I didn't understand why my parents weren't together anymore and I didn't understand why he was telling me a story about the KGB stabbing people to death with syringes. I started to cry, then hyperventilate, and, in a state of mounting panic, Dad invented Ipski-Pipski, the dashing, adventurous young man who became the mainstay of my bedtime stories from then on.

Ipski-Pipski was amazingly talented. Before bed, Dad would ask me what I wanted Ipski-Pipski to be that night. If I said, "A fireman!" Ipski-Pipski smelled smoke and rushed off to find a skyscraper in flames. If I said, "An astronaut!" my bed started to shake and Ipski-Pipski and I were seated atop a giant rocket about to take off. Ipski-Pipski could be anything my dad or I dreamed of: a race-car driver, a cowboy, a soldier. There were no limits.

Oftentimes, Dad would go out and leave me with a babysitter I never liked. One night, after Ipski-Pipski had climbed Mount Everest and Dad went to a party, I realized that I, too, could do anything I wanted to do, so I took Max the dog and left. I wasn't tired, particularly after the Everest assault, and I wanted to find my own mountain to climb. Max, a forty-pound Airedale, understood me. He eyed the door and wagged his tail, and as soon as we got out on the street he started pulling me toward the Hollywood Hills. But Max was also jacked up on Ipski-Pipski stories. He'd been listening every night and wanted to have his own adventures. I was a liability for him. Before we'd reached the end of the block, he was gone, galloping ecstatically toward the HOLLYWOOD sign.

I hadn't brought any mountaineering equipment with me. No peanut butter and jelly, no celery, no ice cream. All I had was my Superman pajamas with the crinkly plastic feet. I needed to stock up on supplies, so I walked down Santa Monica Boulevard until I found a liquor store.

"I need some ice cream," I said to the man behind the counter. He was bearded, unsmiling, and backed by a wall of pint-sized bottles of whisky. "I'm going to climb that mountain." I pointed out the door into the night.

He glanced outside and saw nothing. He seemed surprised and asked me if I was alone. I told him my dog had run away, my dad was at a party, and my babysitter was a member of the KGB.

"Is that right?" he said, smiling for the first time. "And what kind of ice cream is best for mountain climbing?" I didn't hesitate: vanilla Klondike. Very good for going up hills. He dug two cones out of his freezer, dialed 911, and asked me how many mountains I had climbed already. This would be my first, I said, and described how Ipski-Pipski had climbed Everest.

When the cops arrived, I was just at the part where Ipski-Pipski was crawling, inch by inch, toward the summit. I had decided to eat one of the cones—I had two, after all. The cops looked tired and unhappy. Max was trying to dig a hole in the backseat of their squad car and they wanted to get him out of there as soon as possible.

"Come back sometime and finish the story during the daytime," the bearded man said. "I'm always here if you need more supplies."

I waved to him as the cops drove me away. I was having a great adventure—meeting new people, riding around in police cars, and eating ice cream. Unfortunately, Max wanted ice cream as well and snatched the second cone out of my hand. I started yelling at him for being such a stupid dog but was distracted by the sight of my dad and all the neighbors waiting for me in front of our apartment building. Dad pulled me out of the car and hugged me hard while trying to wipe away tears.

"Why are you crying, Daddy?"

"Never, ever do that again," he said in his you're-in-big-trouble tone of voice. "Never leave the house without an adult."

"But you told me I can do anything, just like Ipski-Pipski."

"You can, sweetheart. Just not when you're five."

"Then, when?"

"Later. Now you've got to go straight back to bed."

As I tried to fall asleep that night, I imagined all the great things I could do when I wasn't five. I could fly the fastest airplane, ride a rhinoceros, and paint myself blue like my walls so I'd be invisible in my room. I could hire my own babysitters and tell them that I was allowed to lock them in the broom closet and that my bedtime was one in the morning. I comforted myself with the knowledge that someday I would be old enough to be like Ipski-Pipski.

The promise that we can be anything we want to be is an American ideal. We live in the land of opportunity, and, as a nation, we believe in individuality. We tell our children that they can grow up to be champions if they really put their minds to it.

But is it true? Did I ever have a shot at basketball stardom? My dad took me to the courts religiously when I visited him. I'd try to bounce the ball between my legs and I'd smash myself in the nuts. Passes would plonk me in the head, and I almost never made a basket. I needed glasses from a young age but nobody picked up on it. They just thought I was slow with my hands.

The sad truth is that we can't all be in the NBA. There's no way I could even make it on a semipro baseball team. I'll never be in the Olympics, I wouldn't be allowed near a football field, and when I tried hockey at age six, I was nearly run over by the Zamboni. But my father never stopped telling me that I could succeed. He picked me up, held me above his head so that I could dunk, and told me that soon I'd discover what it was that made me an individual.

But individuality can be hard to come by when there are 280 million other would-be individuals in the country. In practical terms, we first need to figure out when we've achieved uniqueness. We need some way of comparing ourselves to others to prove that we are different. That's why I've always been attracted to competition. Rankings give me a way of knowing how close (or far) I am from being a champion. For instance, I quickly realized that I wouldn't make it to the NBA: I never won even a single game of HORSE. I like to think that was largely due to the fact that I couldn't see the net, but, either way, I was never attached to the NBA per se. For me, the implicit promise of America was that I could be the best at something. It didn't matter what.

So I started with basketball and it didn't work out for me. No big deal. I moved on to hockey and then baseball. As I grew older, the options whittled down. I checked all the big sports off the list by the time I got to high school and was forced to mine a new vein: exploration. Charting new territory had distinguished Columbus, Drake, and Cook; maybe it could work for me. I bought an ice ax and a compass and started hiking.

But the more I climbed, the more I realized that just about everything had been charted. You used to be able to start walking and, before long, arrive at the edge of the map. Now there is no edge. Our generation of explorers is relegated to trying the fourth route on a thrice-climbed spire in the Bugaboos. Thousands have climbed the tallest mountains, so our thirst to be first forces us to fragment the already explored. We have to pretend that being the first to summit the left side of a mountain is just as edifying as being the first to summit it period. The world has run out of challenges, so we've had to invent new ones.

As a nation, we're really good at this kind of invention. We've come up with competitive cup stacking, turned poker into a televised event, and set new records for pumpkin hurling. I don't think it's a coincidence that the present explosion of nontraditional sports coincides with our emergence as the world's only superpower. America used to be a young country. We had unlimited potential and frontiers to explore. We were destined to be the most powerful nation on earth. Well, we've achieved that, so now we've got to do something else with all our energy. We need something new to inspire the kids. Enter cup stacking. It's absurd but it fulfills a deeply American need to accomplish what hasn't already been done.

America's push to invent new challenges came at just the right time for me. When I graduated college, I was in a panic. I had given up mountaineering and was running out of things to try. I eventually took a job as a data entry clerk and began to tell myself that maybe the American dream was dead. Maybe I wasn't meant to be great at something. Maybe I was just supposed to be a subpar data entry clerk.

But then the spirit of Ipski-Pipski came back into my life in a most unusual way.

Lukasz Glowala

CHAPTER ONE

TEAM
USA

Grip up!" the ref shouts at me. I am about to face Rabadanov Rebadan—a.k.a. the Russian Ripper—at the World Armwrestling Federation World Championship in Gdynia, Poland. Rebadan is a dark-eyed, hulking torso with emaciated legs. He is one of Russia's best lightweight armwrestlers and has a reputation for ferocity. Rumor on the floor of this cavernous, Soviet-style gym has it that the Ripper has broken more arms than any other wrestler, and his coach—a gold-toothed man with a blunt, broken nose—is frantically encouraging more such violence. Rebadan snaps his head to the side. I hear his neck crack despite the roar from the thirteen hundred people in the crowd and the jostling of a half dozen photographers. My plan is working. I can tell Rebadan is worried. Or at least confused.

His eyes crisscross my body, looking for weak points. He frowns. All he sees are weak points. I've got bony arms, glasses, and strange, spiky rust-red hair that I point menacingly in his direction. It doesn't make any sense to him. He's never heard of me. Nobody has.

I'm a five-foot-nine-inch, 129-pound data entry clerk from San Francisco named Joshua Davis.

The Ripper slaps himself across the face, willing himself to focus on me. He's wondering what he's missing. He blinks. Most of the faces in the crowd also scrutinize me and seem to be asking the same question: "How the hell did this guy get here?"

Well, I earned it.

Sort of.

To most people, the Mojave Desert looks dry and desolate. For me, it's full of memories. It reminds me of cigarettes, the piss jar, and hours of wordless mind-melding with a Scottish terrier named Ernest. We'd usually head out of L.A. in the afternoon. It was the late seventies and my mom and her best friend, Carole, acted like they were already famous. They were beautiful, on the cusp of being discovered, and with their billowing scarves and oversized shades, they looked like stars, at least to me.

I was just the kid so I got jammed into the Mercedes's luggage space with Ernest, unseen to the world. The car was a flashy two-seater convertible—Mom and Carole looked great in it but it didn't leave me and the dog a lot of room. Ernest coped by sleeping a lot, though periodically he got carsick and vomited on me. I focused on the future. It didn't smell like dog vomit and Mom's cigarettes. In the future, Mom was the movie star she wanted to be, Carole found a man who wouldn't be mean to her, and we drove a much bigger car.

In the present, though, nobody was smiling. A trip to Vegas wasn't about gambling for us. Grandma and Grandpa lived in a trailer behind the Tropicana Hotel. Carole grew up on the outskirts of town. This was a trip home and it was always tense. Carole didn't get along with her parents and Grandpa never seemed happy to see us.

Grandma was excited, but she had learned to mute her feelings around her husband. She came from a blue-blooded East Coast family and majored in French at Middlebury College in the thirties. Her attention was focused on Europe until she met Grandpa, a gardener in New York who had big plans. There was a new town in the western desert, he explained, and it was going to be big. He was handsome and self-assured. He wanted to turn the desert green. She had just read *Candide* and took the closing advice to heart: *"Il faut cultiver notre jardin."* She fell in love and they ran off to start a nursery in Vegas just after World War II.

Mom dreamed big, too. It wasn't hard for her. She was the oldest of six kids and had inherited ambition and good looks. But, despite having married a well-educated woman (or maybe because of that), Grandpa refused to send Mom to college. He encouraged his first son instead and Mom was forced to find another outlet for her ambition.

She started with the local Miss Helldorado beauty contest and won it when she was seventeen. She went on to win Miss Nevada the next year, and got sent to Miami for the 1962 Miss USA contest. It was her big break. She was getting out of Vegas. She was going to be a star. She was nineteen years old.

After two days in Miami, the judges selected fifteen semifinalists, and Mom was one of them. Stardom was within reach. Backstage, the fifteen lined up to have their hair done for the final round. The hairdresser assigned to my mom thought it would be a good idea to do a poofy, flipped-up modern look. Mom had misgivings, but she was young and the hairdresser was a professional. She decided to trust his judgment.

When she walked onstage, she exuded confidence, but her hair sent a different message. It said, "I'm an alien space being." The sheer size of it made her face look small and oppressed, as if she were simply the host for the creature living on top of her head. There was such an aesthetic separation between her and her hair that it was still easy to appreciate her beauty. The judges smiled at her, but then their eyes darted up above her forehead and doubt crossed their faces.

MISS NEVADA

for

MISS UNIVERSE

Official Programme

2:30 P. M.

JUNE 14, 1963

Thunderbird HOTEL

Las Vegas, Nevada

50¢

photo by Toni Garcia

JANET HADLAND — Miss Nevada 1962

Toni Garcia

She didn't win. She didn't even get second. She was the fourth runner-up, and for her it was worse to have had a taste of glory, to have been that close. Of the five finalists, she was the first called to center stage. She was asked to stand on the bottom step while the other three runners-up were announced and led to the higher steps. And finally, Miss USA was crowned right in front of her eyes.

It was a defeat that stayed with my mom for the rest of her life. She took little satisfaction in the four-foot trophy they gave her. Instead, she developed an almost frantic need to get to some finish line first. She chased it for the next twenty years in New York and Los Angeles but always slinked back home through the Mojave as a runner-up. She was in *Vogue, Life,* and *New Woman,* but was never the cover girl. She landed a part in *Funny Girl*, but they made her wear a hat made out of a bushel of wheat and told her it was a nonspeaking role. It didn't help that she split up with my dad when I was three. She was always almost happy, almost successful—always the runner-up.

It gnawed at her. So much so that she began prepping me at a very young age to be a champion. She wanted me to do what she couldn't. She said it was because she was trying to give me the opportunities that she never had, but somehow I always knew that it came down to that moment on the stage in Miami in 1962. The photograph of the contestants hung as a reminder in the darkest part of our hallway. The trophy was kept hidden in storage.

To my mom's credit, she didn't specify which field I was going to be a champion in, though she did obsess about my posture and teach me to walk a fashion runway. But she never told me what to be. She just waited for my particular genius to manifest itself.

She waited, waited some more, and then started to get frustrated. By age six, I wasn't demonstrating any particular genius or even heightened physical skills. I liked hiding. I was particularly good at concealing myself beneath piles of laundry, but, because I was so good at it, she never appreciated that talent.

And so we would roll through the dry late-afternoon smog into the desert to present ourselves in front of Grandpa's severe, silent gaze. Mom wanted to get there and back as fast as possible, so we pissed in a jar and drove a hundred miles per hour. The Mojave was a blur of tumbleweeds, a mason jar of yellow-orange piss, and cigarette ash.

When Grandpa died in 1992, the Mojave took over his role. It stared at me with unblinking, disappointed, burned-out gray eyes. My mother still believed in me—she had nothing else to pin her hopes on—but hope in the desert is usually called a mirage. The desert had given up on me a long time ago, so I kept my distance from it.

Then, two years ago, I got trapped. I had driven to Telluride, Colorado, from San Francisco to visit a friend and now the friend asked if I could take him to L.A. on my way back. I had been his guest and couldn't say no. It would have been too difficult to explain why I didn't want to drive through the Mojave. Plus, I figured that we'd be talking the whole time and I wouldn't even notice where I was.

I could feel it approaching as we descended through Utah. The air dried out and the desert began to suck all the moisture out of me, as if it wanted to sift me down into a pile of dust to show me what I was really worth. My friend fell asleep. I poked him in the ribs, but he kept sleeping. I was left alone with the desert.

I knew I wasn't worth much. I had eight hundred dollars in my checking account and the balance kept dropping. I had quit my job as a data entry clerk at the local phone company to try, one last time, to find something I was great at. I decided to try journalism—maybe I could be a Woodward or a Bernstein—but I was only making about two hundred a month writing for a free weekly paper in San Francisco. My first big assignment was to write a review of San Francisco's best strip clubs.

Tara, my wife, was not pleased and wouldn't let me go to the clubs during business hours. I viewed the assignment as my big break but was forced to do my reporting first thing in the morning, when no one but the droopy-eyed managers were around. My reporting was limited to comments about the menu: "At BoyToys you can munch vanilla plantain prawns while watching continuous strip shows!" I was far from success. Very far.

Though I had given in to her reporting constraints, Tara was still not happy. We lived in a 250-square-foot apartment that received no direct sunlight. I wrote my articles underneath our dorm-room-style lofted bed. She wanted the American dream—a nice home, a regular income, and a gainfully employed, respectable husband. That wasn't me, and heading into the Mojave only made that reality starker and more painful.

I pulled off the road and stopped at a diner in Needles, California. I needed some water—everything about me felt dry. As I walked through the doorway, I noticed a flyer advertising "Dennis Quaid and the Sharks." I stopped to look (Dennis Quaid had a band?) and, underneath, a second flyer announced the upcoming U.S. National Armwrestling Championship in Laughlin, Nevada. The words "Anybody can compete—no entry requirements" jumped out at me.

I could almost hear my grandpa whisper into my ear: "You'll never amount to much." In the forties, Grandpa had been in the right place at the right time—Vegas was about to boom and needed a man like him. But he wasn't a good businessman and rarely got the lucrative accounts. He watched as other gardeners came to town and turned the desert green. He sat on the sidelines and did small jobs. He was there first, had seen the potential, but couldn't deliver.

Now, in my mind, he was telling me that I couldn't deliver either. I was desperate, and the Mojave made me vulnerable. Thank goodness I didn't see a flyer for a bug-eating contest because at that moment I realized that I was going to be an armwrestler. I had a strong premonition that it was my long-awaited, undiscovered talent.

Even if I didn't win, it would make Tara look at me differently. I could be a macho man—at least for a day. And simply by doing something that I probably shouldn't, I felt like I was going to make a point to both my mother and my buried grandpa. As long as I was trying, there was still a chance that I could redeem my mom's loss and silence my grandpa's doubt.

Tara was incredulous.

"Have you gone completely insane?" she said when I got home and told her my plan. "Do you want a broken arm? What am I going to do with a one-armed husband?"

She's really beautiful when she's angry. Her intelligent, dark brown eyes narrow and she stands a little taller with the indignation, pushing her breasts out. I told her she looked good.

"Don't try to smart-mouth your way out of this," she warned, using the tone of voice she used on the errant fifteen-year-olds she taught in a local high school. "I'm wise to your tricks."

It was true. It's hard to play games with a woman you've known since you were sixteen. We met in high school, fell in love in college, and got married a few years after graduation. But she knows me well enough to know that she doesn't fully understand me and probably never will.

"You need to be looking at the classifieds," she muttered, losing steam. "Not running off to armwrestle in the desert."

She knew it was useless. I wasn't going to change my mind. Her teaching job covered our rent and expenses, so, as much as it annoyed her, we could afford this. I told her that I needed to keep trying to find something I was good at. If I just gave up and took any old job, I'd be as unhappy as I was at the phone company and it would be no fun to be married to me.

"But why armwrestling?" she pleaded, pointing out that I'd never armwrestled in my life.

"Exactly! I could be great and just never knew it," I said.

"Honey, I'm sorry but it's just really, really unlikely," she said, eyeing my bone-thin arms. "You'll win when hell freezes over."

Two weeks later, I fueled up the baby-blue Buick LeSabre we had inherited from Tara's grandma and headed back out into the desert. Tara had to teach, so I was on my own in the 115-degree heat. The dryness didn't bother me as much this time. I felt more secure now that I had a goal. And without a coating of dog vomit the trip seemed easy.

According to the flyer, the event was at the Avi Resort and Casino, a multistory, pyramid-shaped building in the middle of a scrub-brush expanse. The Avi's main electronic sign broadcasted the words FUN IN THE SUN and LOOSE SLOTS, but no armwrestling. A smaller sign trumpeted $1 BINGO. I scrutinized my flyer and checked the date. There was no doubt about it: this was the right place and the right time.

But inside, nobody knew about the armwrestling nationals. I asked at the reception desk, but the man behind the counter had no idea what I was talking about. As my frustration rose, he asked a colleague and she thought something might be going on "out back."

I found a large, unmarked shed behind the casino. It looked like an industrial greenhouse, though the material bent across the arching exterior was thick white plastic. Its most obvious entrance was locked, so I walked around it and pushed open a side door. Two folding picnic tables sat on a three-foot-high stage at the end of the shed. An American flag was stapled to the wall and large men with massive biceps paced nervously along the walls. This was the U.S. National Armwrestling tournament.

Denise Wattles, the secretary-general of the U.S. Armwrestling Federation, waved at me from the stage. "Shut the door," she shouted. Wattles was a pudgy, bespectacled woman from Montana in her late forties who wore her dirty-blond hair in dense ringlets. "We're having air-conditioning problems," she said.

I shut the door quickly and Wattles advised me to weigh in. She pointed toward a battered doctor's office scale and a man drinking a beer told me to step up. He held a clipboard and wore jeans with a black-and-white referee shirt. He flicked the counterbalance around until the scale showed that I weighed 127 pounds. I was two pounds off my normal weight—the desert had already sucked moisture out of me. "You're in the lightweight division," the referee said dismissively. "Wait till we call your name and then come back up here and wrestle." He pronounced it "rassle."

I hovered around an armwrestling practice table set up beside the stage and tried not to show how anxious I was. Like most people, I had jokingly armwrestled when I was a kid, but I'd never had a serious match. I didn't even know that there was such a thing as a regulation armwrestling table. I thought you just plopped your elbow down on a table and wrestled.

It was much more organized than that. First of all, you stood to wrestle. The four-posted metal table was about stomach height and had pads for the elbows and on either side where the arm would hit the table for a win or a loss. Handgrips made out of metal jutted up on the left and right sides of the table.

A group of three middleweight guys in tank tops were gathered around the table and watching two large men warm up. The warm-up involved armwrestling in slow motion. It looked like a dance. Roll right, roll left, roll right. Their expressions were blank, but after a minute they smiled, laughed, and thanked each other.

"Hey, I'm new to this," I said to the tank top next to me. He looked to be in his early thirties and his shirt was from last year's nationals, so I figured he knew a thing or two. "Could you give me some tips?"

"Sure, why not?" he said easily and motioned at the now empty table.

It's a very intimate thing to hold another man's hand for an extended period of time, particularly when you've never met him. My newfound instructor gripped my hand with surprising delicacy. I could feel him sizing me up just by the way he responded to my grip. For each small change in the pressure I applied, the muscles in his hand adjusted and his fingers rippled across my knuckles.

"I'm Josh, by the way," I said.

"Rick Soliwada. Erie, Pennsylvania," he said. "One-hundred-forty-five-pound right and left silver medal at last year's world championship."

"You must be good," I said. He looked much bigger than 145 pounds. I would have guessed 170, but I might have been influenced by his unkempt dark hair, big nose, and aura of calm assurance.

"God created me to be an armwrestler," Rick said matter-of-factly. "He gave me long, big forearms, big hands. He set me up."

And with that, Rick slammed my hand down on the pad. It felt mechanical, like a metal press had just smushed my arm. Rick smiled.

It turns out that he had just gotten off the bus from Erie. He had spent fifty-two hours on a Greyhound to get to Nevada and was due back on the bus the next morning to head home. It didn't bother him—he told me that he was sure he was going to win the national championship for the second time. This was, after all, why God put him here on this planet. He didn't have a lot of money—he worked construction part-time—but God had created Greyhound and Greyhound was affordable enough to let him fulfill his destiny.

I, on the other hand, did not appear to be created for armwrestling. Rick said that everything about my form was terrible. He showed me how to stay "locked-up" so that my arm acted as a lever for my body, allowing me to throw my full weight into a "pull." Then he explained armwrestling strategy.

First, you size up your opponent. If you think you are stronger than he is, you twist your wrist so that your fingernails face you. This is known as the "hook." Theoretically, it traps your opponent in your power spot. You can then throw your shoulder behind your arm and focus the full effect of your muscle and weight against him. It's called the "inside move" because you're leaning into the table.

But if you think your opponent is stronger, you go for the outside move, a.k.a. the "top roll" or "going over the top." In this move, you lean away from the table and twist your hand away so that you see your knuckles. The goal is to pull your opponent's arm away from his body and, therefore, away from his strength.

"But if you top roll, you might get your arm broken," Rick concluded. He explained that I should never turn perpendicular to the table. "That's when you'll get snapped."

Denise Wattles passed by and thanked Soliwada for helping me out. She was like the den mother and made the event feel like a family affair. She knew all the wrestlers' names, stood on her tiptoes to give them hugs when they arrived, and asked how their families were doing.

"We've got a real star here this year," she said to me, pointing at a well-groomed man across the room. "That's Jeff Thomchesson, the world champion. He could teach you a lot, too."

Thomchesson's arms probably weighed about seventy-five pounds each and were clad in bright yellow arm warmers. He was a handsome, mustachioed man attended to by a petite brunette who scampered around him, shaking his arms and rubbing his shoulders while he sat regally in a folding plastic chair.

Rick was starting to get "nic fits"—he told me he quits smoking before every tournament to make him meaner—and he walked away without saying goodbye. It was getting hot inside the room and I could feel tensions rising. But Thomchesson looked relaxed, so I walked over and introduced myself.

The champion cordially motioned to a chair next to him and told me to have a seat. He had a calm, confident manner and seemed eager to share his thoughts with me. "People have misconceptions about this sport," Thomchesson began. "They think it's all about big guys tearing each other's arms off."

I nodded my head in agreement. That's pretty much what I thought about it.

"But that's completely wrong. You're going to see some guys here today who look like they're physically incapable of armwrestling and they're just awesome."

That boded well for me. I asked him if armwrestling was more about technique than about brute strength and if he thought technique could be learned quickly.

"Listen, armwrestling is a very complex sport. There's no reason it shouldn't be in the Olympics if Ping-Pong is in there."

I wasn't aware that Ping-Pong was an Olympic sport, but I didn't question him. He had warmed to his subject and was enthusiastically telling me that most of the guys here trained three to five times a week and should be considered world-class athletes. Thomchesson's personal regimen included working out four times a week in a specially outfitted armwrestling gym in Texas.

"I tell you what," he said with a Texan twang. "If you really want to learn, you come out to Texas and train with us. We've got some machines that will turn you into a darn good armwrestler."

Denise tapped on her microphone. "Okay, boys, it's time to wrestle."

"You're welcome to come anytime," Thomchesson said. He wished me luck and then stood to shake out what he referred to as the "big guns."

I looked around and noticed that the shed had filled up. There were about sixty people sitting in the folding chairs in front of the stage. It was also getting ridiculously hot. It was 114 degrees outside. Without air-conditioning, we could die, but Denise wasn't overly concerned.

"I'd like to welcome everyone to the U.S. National Armwrestling Championship," Denise said. "I apologize about the air-conditioning. They tell me it's broken, but that's okay. It'll keep everyone's muscles loose. Just be sure to drink a lot of water."

She placed the mike in front of what looked like her clock radio, pressed a button, and Cher began to sing the national anthem. Everyone stood up and faced the flag stapled to the wall.

The song ended to a roar of claps and hollers. "You ready to armwrestle?" Denise shouted into the mike. A lady in the crowd stood up and let out an approving shriek. Denise began reading names and the U.S. nationals got under way.

My name was quickly called and I walked onstage for the first armwrestling match of my life. A wiry guy wearing a backward baseball cap followed me up and politely offered his hand for a gentlemanly prematch shake. His grip was relaxed and his movements were fluid. He had clearly done this before and appeared subdued and comfortable. I thought the handshake was a nice touch—before every match, opponents are expected to shake. To my mind, it dignifies the sport. It may be known as a drunken barroom pursuit, but at this level armwrestling was about honor and decorum.

Remembering what Rick had taught me, I grabbed the post with my left hand and "gripped up" with the guy under the slightly intoxicated eyes of the referee. When the ref abruptly shouted, "Go!" I felt like I was standing in the midst of an explosion. My arm was wrenched over, and before I could react, he smashed my hand into the table. I was thankful there was a pad there.

It was a double-elimination event so I wasn't too upset. I was still in the running, and I'm a fast learner. As the matches progressed, I studied the different styles and made mental notes. I drank lots of water.

When I was called for my second match, I had to pee but was

pleased to see a guy even smaller than me on the other side of the table. We shook hands and then gripped up. I decided to go for the hook, and when the ref signaled the start, I held him in the middle. It was thrilling. I wasn't overwhelmed like before.

I'm doing it! I thought. *I'm holding my own.*

And then, slowly, my arm started fading backward. I gasped for air and tried to pull harder but nothing happened. The little guy glanced up at me, as if to see if I'd had enough, and then he pushed me smoothly down to the pad. I was beat.

I walked off the stage in a depressed daze. What was I going to say to Tara? She would tell me that I needed to grow up and stop chasing my dreams, that I needed to start acting my age and take on some responsibility instead of spending weekends lost in the middle of the desert with a bunch of armwrestlers.

I started drinking Budweisers and watched from the audience as Thomchesson and Soliwada crushed all their opponents. I chastised myself for not listening more closely. I knew I could have won that second match if I had only locked-up like Rick said.

The matches ended and Denise picked up her microphone. "And now we're going to do the awards ceremony," she said. She sat next to a large folding table covered with medals and trophies. "Starting with the lightweight division, for fourth place in the United States, we have Joshua Davis. Come on up here, Josh."

It took me a second to realize she was talking about me. "Joshua, you out there?" Denise said, tapping her microphone to make sure it was working.

"I'm coming," I shouted and leaped up. Everybody clapped warmly for me. When I got to the stage, Denise handed me a medal. It turned out that there were only three other competitors in the division. I was fourth out of four. But that still made me the fourth-highest-ranked lightweight armwrestler in the United States.

I drove home a happy man. When I walked through the doorway of our gloomy apartment, I was wearing the medal. Tara thought I had bought it, but I soon convinced her that I had won it fair and square. I made her squeeze my biceps. She was impressed, and we made love on the floor.

Four weeks later, I got a call from Leonard Harkless, the president of the U.S. Armwrestling Association. I had met him briefly in Laughlin, but we hadn't talked much. Now he wanted to know how I was feeling, how my arm was doing. I was surprised to hear from him, and told him I was doing fine. In truth, my arm was still sore but I didn't want to sound like a wimp.

Harkless coughed awkwardly and then explained that the bylaws of the association dictated that the first- and second-place finishers in each division at nationals were invited to compete at the world championship. If either couldn't attend, Harkless worked his way down the rankings.

"And, uh, you're next in line" he stammered. "The second- and third-place guys can't go. Can you make it?"

I felt a warm glow spread through me. Not only was I the fourth-ranked lightweight armwrestler in the United States, I was now going to have a shot at the world title. *Damn straight, I'm interested.*

"Well, you've got two months to get ready," Harkless said skeptically. "Welcome to Team USA."

As he was about to hang up, I remembered to ask where the championship was held.

"Gdynia, Poland," he said. "Northern Poland. In December. Buy yourself some long johns."

I had to get started immediately. I took out a piece of paper and jotted down a three-pronged strategy. First, I needed to find a coach. Then, I'd need to put on some serious muscle, and, finally, develop a look.

The look would be the underpinning of the whole enterprise— once I *looked* menacing, I would *feel* menacing. Plus, I didn't want to repeat the mistake my mother had made in 1962. I wasn't going to leave anything to chance or bad hair. So I started by calling Rari Acosta, a San Francisco stylist recommended by a friend. I explained my situation (skinny, prone to book reading) and asked him what he could do. He looked at his schedule and told me to come in the following morning.

Rari worked at a salon in San Francisco's Cole Valley, a yuppieish neighborhood on the slope above Haight-Ashbury. He wore his black hair in a ponytail down to the middle of his back, had a compass tattooed on his neck, and generally looked like a very gay pirate. He sat me down and walked around me twice without saying anything.

"Oh, my god, I've got it," he said, mussing up my shaggy dirty-blond hair. "We're going rust red. I can see it. You'll look really mean."

An hour and a half later, I walked out a little unsure of myself, my head an unusual ball of spiky red hair. But people on the street did look at me warily, which I took to be a good sign.

I got home and dialed Jeff Thomchesson in Houston. He had also qualified for the world championship (much less of a surprise, of course) and seemed like the ideal coach if he was still willing to train me.

"San Francisco's just not the place for it," I told him.

"Sure, we'd love to," he said affably. "We got a whole lot of pullers down here, big and small. We also got a tournament coming up for money. Why don't you come out for that?"

I had a frequent-flier ticket on Southwest and told Tara that the whole trip wouldn't cost more than a hundred dollars. I explained that it was absolutely necessary if I wanted to prevent bodily harm to myself at the world championship. She agreed that I needed more training. "A lot more," she said.

I got to Houston on the night of the tournament and met Thomchesson in the parking lot of The Seashore, a Gulf-side bar with a rowdy crowd. It also happened to be Halloween, so an assortment of extraterrestrials, cowboys, cavewomen, and red devils milled around the parking lot.

Jeff had just arrived in his diminutive Honda and was wrapped head to foot in Saran wrap. He looked like a mummy in the passenger seat. His girlfriend, Stephanie—the petite woman with him in Laughlin—ran around the car to help him out and began pulling off the layers of plastic.

"I was a few pounds over," Thomchesson explained as Stephanie pulled the plastic off by running circles around him, revealing a well-muscled man wearing boxer shorts. I could feel hot air billowing out of their car. "I would never do this for a serious event, but for a little fun thing like this, I don't mind getting wrapped up."

"We turned the heat all the way up in the car," Stephanie said proudly, "and I bet you he lost at least three or four pounds on the drive over."

"It's like my own little portable sauna," Jeff added.

Once Jeff got some clothes on we walked into the bar, located on a large, partially covered deck overlooking a shipping channel. At a rickety armwrestling table set up beside a fake pond, a woman dressed as Tinker Bell was wrestling a horned she-devil.

"Come sit with us," said a man wearing a plush shark on his head. He was sitting with three bikini-clad women in their forties and was slurring his words. "We're here to get fucked-up," one of the women said, introducing herself.

I asked them if they were also there to armwrestle and Shark Man said he didn't know anything about the tournament. One of the bikinied women leaned over him, her boobs spilling out of an inadequate bikini.

"Where'd you get hair like that?" she demanded.

"Y'all don't know who this is?" Jeff said, appearing behind me after signing up for the tournament. "This here's the newest member of the U.S. armwrestling team. Y'all better treat him nice."

I got lots of free drinks after that, which contributed to the loss of all my matches. I wrestled a guy who was in charge of pressing the shut-down button at the local electrical plant. He brought a bungee cord to work, tied it to his chair, and built his tendon strength while he waited for disaster. I wrestled a telephone repairman who told me that it was the steroids that made his arms nearly as big around as my waist. I even wrestled Jeff, who carried on a lively conversation with a few people beside the table while I struggled with his arm. Even when he let me use both hands, I couldn't budge him.

"Feel the steel," he said and continued chatting with his friends.

After Jeff won the tournament, Stephanie drove us back to their place and told me I could sleep on their couch. They lived in a one-bedroom apartment with three cats and twenty-eight armwrestling trophies, one of which was nearly as big as Stephanie. An armwrestling table dominated their bedroom and the walls were lined with pictures of Jeff armwrestling.

We stayed up all night talking about armwrestling technique. Around two, Jeff started telling me about his past. He said that his mother abandoned him beside a dumpster when he was a baby. He was eventually adopted by a nice family but developed a lot of anger when they told him the truth at the end of high school. He channeled that anger into his armwrestling and was headed for an international title in his early twenties when the anger got the best of him. He wouldn't tell me what happened but he ended up in prison.

He didn't armwrestle for a decade after that and only got back into it four years ago when he met Gary Ray, whose gym we were going to in the morning. Gary convinced him to give the sport another try and coached him to last year's world championship.

"Getting back into armwrestling gave me a second chance to put my life back together," Jeff said, patting Stephanie's knee. "Hey, just look at her. We met at my first bar tournament."

"I was just there for a drink," Stephanie noted. "And then all these armwrestlers showed up."

I told them about Tara, and how she wanted me to settle down. I explained that I was running out of time and really wanted to find something I was great at. Jeff said I had a lot of heart, and if I was able to channel it into my forearm, I had a bright future in the sport. We wouldn't know until we got to Poland, but Jeff said he believed in me.

By three, we decided to call it a night. Jeff shook my hand and gave me the burly man's hug—a sort of combination handshake/pat-on-the-back/chest-thump. I was no longer just a member of Team USA on paper—I was one of the guys.

In the morning, it was made abundantly clear to me that, while I was indeed one of the guys, I stood out as one of the smallest, skinniest, and weakest guys. Jeff drove me over to Gary's house, a single-story 1960s home in a blue-collar Houston suburb. Gary, an affable, stout man in his mid-fifties, was a road-construction foreman and knew how to build things. In his spare time, he had assembled what he claimed was the world's largest armwrestling training facility in his two-car garage. Gary had welded almost every piece of equipment himself and devised one-of-a-kind training machines.

There was a machine for building elbow-tendon strength. One contraption was made from the remains of an old steam engine—it built "radial wrist strength." The ceiling was lined with monkey bars and rock-climbing holds, and a stack of cannonballs sat in one corner. Gary picked up a cannonball and lobbed it to me. I caught it with both hands and let out a grunt. He told me to toss it up and down in one hand and roll it around the outside of my fingers. He demonstrated, manipulating the thirty-pound ball of iron as if it were a tennis ball. I held it in one hand for about a second before my other hand had to fly in for backup.

Then Gary strapped me into a homemade machine that Jeff called "The Wrestle-ator." This device was a system that looked like a movie projector with weights strung over the projection reels. Once my hand was secured, I could feel the backward pull just as if someone were trying to pin me. I struggled against it and managed to slam down my fake opponent's nonexistent hand.

"Good job," Gary said. He unstrapped me and told me to climb the monkey bars on his ceiling five times. He ran me through the machines built for enhancing wrist strength, tendon resilience, and triceps growth. By noon, I couldn't lift my arms.

Gary's wife came in with plates of chili dogs. Though I was ravenous, I begged off. The chili had meat in it, I delicately explained, and I was a vegetarian.

"I've never met a vegetarian armwrestler," Gary said, incredulous.

"Well, then, I'm the first," I said proudly.

Since I had wrestled right-handed at nationals, I was only going to compete right-handed in Poland. That meant that I needed to focus on getting the right side of my body huge while emaciating the left in order to stay in the 122-to-132-pound class. When I got home, I began lifting weights, but only with my right arm.

Soon I looked like the Hunchback of Notre Dame. I was eating five meals a day and became obsessed with the idea that if I was late to eat a meal, the jealous left side of my body would take the opportunity to cannibalize the thick muscles on my right side.

At night, as I was trying to fall asleep, I began to visualize armwrestling matches and would get so pumped up that I kept myself awake for hours and traumatized Tara with my twitchings. She was already peeved with me because after work and on the weekends I made her wrestle me so I could perfect my technique. I won most of the matches.

"She's probably letting you win," Mom said when I called to brief her on my progress. "And if you can't win every match against your wife, how are you going to handle the Russians or the Poles?"

Mom was fully vested in my ascendancy in the world of armwrestling. She called for daily updates and offered a lot of useless advice, like how to walk on the armwrestling stage ("Gdynia is not Milan, Mom"). She realized that this was likely to be our family's next best shot at gold and wanted to help. We were finally back in reach of a championship. It had been a long time.

Even Tara came around eventually. At the airport, she kissed my biceps for good luck and told me that there was more where those kisses came from as long as I didn't get my arm broken. All the support buoyed me and I arrived in Poland feeling optimistic.

Gdynia, Poland, however, did not inspire optimism. Gray Communist-era buildings and a biting cold wind kept most of Team USA huddled inside the Lucky Hotel, a two-story building that resembled an army barracks. Wrestlers ventured outside only in search of Budweiser (a microbrew of sorts in Poland) and McDonald's, the most likely place in town to see other team members.

I met up with Denise, Rick, Jeff, and Stephanie in the hotel restaurant on the first night. Denise gave me a fancy black Team USA jacket with heavily muscled embroidered arms emblazoned on the left side. On the right, she had "Joshua" sewn in with golden thread. The rest of the team had the same personalized jackets. When I put mine on, Jeff clapped me on the back and said, "Poland sucks."

Jeff was having a hard time. He couldn't sleep, his stomach hurt, he had a headache, and he couldn't eat the food. It was strange to hear such a big man whine. Randy Nelson, a team member from Cincinnati, leaned over from the adjoining table. "You should have brought your own food, like I did," he said to Jeff.

Randy had jam-packed two suitcases with canned pinto beans, spinach, green beans, cereal, and bottles of Slim-Fast. He was afraid that the Poles wouldn't have any food and he didn't want to starve. "I brought enough food," he said, "to survive for over a week."

He offered to cook me dinner—the menu would include a can of beans and some Slim-Fast—but I declined. A bowl of borscht sounded a lot better.

The next morning, we had our first official team meeting in the lobby of the hotel. We went around the circle and introduced ourselves and noted our armwrestling accomplishments. Everybody except me had something to say. I just mentioned my name and told them I was proud to be there.

Though the team didn't quite know what to think of me, they could see that I was committed to the sport, and I think my excitement compensated for any lack of experience. Also, having Jeff's support legitimized me. On a more practical level, as long as I was willing to talk about armwrestling twenty-four hours a day, armwrestlers were an exceedingly welcoming group of people.

Denise had hired tour guides to show us around the area, so we set out on a walking tour of Gdynia. First, we visited the beach, which, at 10 degrees below zero, was not a lot of fun. The wind whipped along the shore, pelting us in the face with frozen sand. Next, we walked the length of Poland's longest wooden pier. At the end of the pier, one of the guides pointed out to sea and explained that a long peninsula enclosed the water in front of us. The historic fishing village of Hel was located at the end of the peninsula.

"Did you say 'Hel'?" I asked through numbed lips.

"Yes," the guide said.

"Is the temperature out there about the same as it is here?"

"Colder, probably."

"So Hel is frozen over?"

"Yes, but in our language, *Hel* means—"

I didn't care what it meant in Polish. I'm an American, and in America Tara had told me that I'd win when hell froze over. Well, it just did.

The morning of the competition, a chartered bus dropped us off behind a large brick building on the outskirts of Gdynia. Inside, a stage was set up on the far side of a full-length basketball court and gargantuan men from twenty-nine countries milled around sizing one another up. Each wore a team uniform, ranging from the much-admired embroidered Canadian team jackets to blue T-shirts with the letters "KAZ" chalked on for Team Kazakhstan. Though it was early in the morning, a deafening techno soundtrack blasted from loudspeakers.

The first thing I noticed was at least three burly Russians on crutches with missing or shriveled legs. I realized with a start that these guys—who would normally weigh more than 160—could make my 132-pound weight class because of their missing limbs. I thought about turning around—it wasn't too late. I could go on a tour of northern Poland, visit Hel, have some fun. But when I saw the expression on Jeff's face, I knew I'd stay. He looked like he was about to throw up. If the world champion was having problems, then it was okay for me to be scared, too.

We sat down in the bleachers and tried to cheer one another up. Randy Nelson gave me a bottle of Slim-Fast. Rick Soliwada handed me a yellow, minty-smelling bottle emblazoned with a picture of a horse. "It's a muscle stimulant for horses; rub it into your elbow," he said, pouring a few drops in the crook of my arm.

"Listen to me," Jeff said as a tingling sensation enveloped my right arm. "You're not strong enough to hook any of these guys, so don't even try. Your only hope is to top-roll them, but you got to be careful not to get your arm broken."

He grabbed my hand to go over some final pointers on the top roll. Talking to me calmed him down and I was glad to help him. He'd been training steadily for months and his forearms oozed off his elbow, cascading away from the rest of his arm in layers of muscle. He looked ready to me. I wasn't sure how I looked.

"You gonna make us proud?" barked teammate Iron Mike O'Hara. O'Hara, a brawny, crew-cut guy from Ohio, seemed to scan me for signs of weakness. I tried not to flinch when I noticed that the pink arm warmer he wore to keep his muscles loose was smeared with the blood of a vanquished opponent.

"Armwrestling is who I am," Iron Mike continued unprompted, implying that I had a ways to go. "People ask me how I learned to wrestle and I ask them how they learned to wipe their ass. It comes naturally to me."

Ten minutes later, when I was called for my first match, I tried not to think of myself as toilet paper. Fortunately, I found myself opposite an elflike Spaniard. I concentrated on looking mean and lowered my head a little to confront him with the full force of my menacing red hair.

He pinned me in less than a tenth of a second. He couldn't have hit the pad any quicker if my arm wasn't there. But maybe it was a fluke. I couldn't discount that. Maybe I just needed another sip of Slim-Fast.

Now, twenty minutes later, I'm fully ready. The horse-muscle stimulant has electrified my arm and I've got Rabadanov Rebadan, the Russian Ripper, in my sights. He might be a national champion in Russia, but this is Poland, where his title carries no weight.

His maniacal coach is screaming in Russian and flashing his gold teeth at me but I'm not bothered. They sense my power and it scares them.

I grab Rebadan's hand and a cloud of chalk erupts. The ref holds our hands steady and I grit my teeth.

This is it. I am ready to destroy. I am an armwrestling machine. I can win this thing.

"READY, GO!"

I'm pinned in two tenths of a second.

And yet I place seventeenth in a field of eighteen. I'm comforted by the fact that some poor wanker actually managed to place below me, but then somebody tells me that he didn't show up. Either way, without ever winning a match I am now ranked in the top eighteen 132-pound armwrestlers in the world. Sometimes, you just can't lose.

General Employment

A $250K-$400K 1st year income. Potential from home. No selling, not MLM. ▓▓▓▓ ▓▓▓▓▓. 24 hr recorded message.

Bullfighting Manager Needed Up and coming local bullfighter seeks manager to handle all aspects of operations. Travel the world and take home a percentage of the winnings ▓▓▓▓▓▓▓

GOVERNMENT HIRING Forestry/Parks/Postal/Firefighters/Police/Secuirty. $35K+ benefits & training. Mon-Fri 9am-10pm/EST. ▓▓▓▓▓▓ ext. ▓▓. (CAL*SCAN)

San Francisco Bay Guardian

CHAPTER TWO

EL AMERICANO
DESESPERADO

I returned home to San Francisco feeling great, though my mom was disappointed. I didn't even make it past fourth runner-up. There was a tightness in her voice when I called to tell her the news, but the stress of being my mom's only child—the only one able to redeem her loss—somehow lifted. I may not have won anything, but I had lived an Ipski-Pipski adventure. For a brief period of time, I had done what I dreamed of doing when I was five.

It made me a happier person. With a newfound clarity, I appreciated the little details of my life that I'd overlooked in my craze to succeed. My mouth watered at the *macchiato*-tinted smoothness of Tara's skin. She's a beguiling blend of Indian and Italian heritage—she was raised in Boston, but her father is from southern India and her mother is Italian-American. The mix produced a beautiful, no-nonsense woman and I realized afresh that I was lucky to be married to her.

Tara was proud of my accomplishment but it wasn't long before the old issues resurfaced. Despite being an internationally ranked armwrestler, I still didn't have a job. I also understood that I probably wasn't going to make it as a professional armwrestler. In fact, I really couldn't hope to ever do much better than I had already done.

So, rather than fade away like so many athletic stars, I decided to retire from armwrestling at my peak. Tara cooked up a nice spaghetti dinner, opened a bottle of wine, and we had a small celebration at our folding table in the living room. That's when she delivered the ultimatums.

"There's three things I want," she said, the wineglasses still vibrating from our toast. "First, I need a bathtub."

"I thought we were celebrating."

"We are. We're celebrating the fact that you've given up the whole Don Quixote thing."

"I never said that."

"Second, I want a proper dining room."

"And it's not a 'Don Quixote thing.' "

"Third, I want direct sunlight."

Our apartment was a critical component of my life plan. It was ridiculously small and the sun only made it in for about fifteen minutes a day in the middle of July. But it was cheap and allowed me to pursue my dreams without too much financial strain. Judging from the determination in Tara's tone, I knew that this was an argument I wasn't going to win at this moment, but I also realized that she never directly said she wanted to move.

When she came back from work the next day, I laid out my plan. I sat her down and handed her a printout from the "Omni Deep-Soaking Japanese-Style Bath" online website. An image showed two people bathing in a three-square-foot stand-up tub. The caption referred to the bath's "cunning dimensions."

"What's this?" she asked.

"If we move the toilet into the shower stall, we can install a cold plunge with the toilet's water hookup," I said. "That takes care of ultimatum number one."

"A cold plunge is not the same thing as a bathtub," she said, already annoyed.

"Then I'll staple reflectors to the side of the building across the way," I said, bringing out the bag full of aluminum foil I had bought earlier in the day. "That'll bounce tons of light in here. It'll be like the beach."

While she looked at the tinfoil with bewilderment, I pushed on. In my sketchbook, I had drawn up plans to build a second floor in our living room. Basically, I planned to turn a room with ten-foot ceilings into two rooms with five-foot ceilings.

"Josh," she said, "we're moving. Did I fail to mention that?"

"You never said *moving.* You said *bathtub, light, dining room.*" I counted them out on my fingers.

"Well, I'm saying it now."

"We can't afford it."

"Then, maybe you should get a job."

"I have a job."

"A job that actually pays money."

"I don't want that kind of job."

"There are some jobs out there that are perfectly interesting, exciting jobs that will pay you money. It's not all bean pushing."

"Bean *counting.*"

"You know what I mean."

"Or paper pushing."

"Josh."

"Give me an example."

"I don't know. I'm not a job counselor. But maybe you should go see one."

Fine. The next morning, I made an appointment to see Bob Fitch, a parent at Tara's high school and a job counselor with a local agency.

When I went in to see the guy, I wasn't impressed. He wore a frayed sports jacket, jeans, and leather sandals and looked to be in his late forties. The room had no windows, a slight buzz from the overhead fluorescent light, and a dry-erase board with the word "Energize!" written in one corner. Fitch looked like he needed some coffee.

"So tell me a little bit about your job history," he said slowly.

I explained that I was a writer but that my wife wanted to move to a bigger apartment so I was going to have to make at least forty thousand dollars a year. Currently, I'd be lucky to clear five grand. "So, basically, I'm willing to consider anything that will get me to the forty-k mark."

"What are your job skills?"

"I can type."

"Typing's good," he said automatically, as if someone had just pulled a string on his back.

"I've also done data entry at the phone company."

"Are you willing to work multiple shifts?" Fitch asked. "Because you could clear forty if you were willing to do data entry seven days a week for double shifts. But you'd have to keep your accuracy up, which can be hard when you're working those kinds of hours."

That sounded really horrific. I was willing to take risks, I said, but not with my mental health. Fitch looked at me intently for a second and then leaned in. "Do you have both of your kidneys?" he asked quietly.

I told him I did.

"Now, I'm not saying I know anybody who could do this, but you could probably get at least twenty to twenty-five k for one of your kidneys."

He had a sly grin on his face. I couldn't tell if he was joking.

"You could almost make it as a writer if you did it," he said. "And it's not like you need two."

"Listen, I'm not selling my kidneys," I said, getting angry.

"I'm not saying you'd sell both of them," he said, laughing.

"Well, I'm saying that I'm not selling either of them."

"Okay, fine. It's your life."

"Exactly," I said, thinking that this guy was truly a crackpot. I started looking for the right way to cut this short.

"I'm just trying to help," he said. "And what I'm seeing is that there is a bit of a disconnect between your skill set and your desired wage. You say you're willing to take risks, you want forty grand a year, and you want to do something that excites you."

"That's about right," I said, still fuming.

"What about a sports mascot? You could be the guy in the shark outfit who does belly flops on the opposing team. Or what about a rodeo clown? That's exciting."

"Would I make forty grand?"

"Probably not. But what about a bullfighter? They probably make good money."

A bullfighter! It was the first intelligent thing he had said. I asked if he had any clients who had gone down that job path and he shook his head. I was the first person he had ever proposed it to.

"You're not my typical client," he said. "And frankly, I'm just grasping at straws here."

Somehow, I walked out of there feeling like the session was worthwhile. I didn't know much about bullfighting, but I knew that matadors were a big deal in Europe. It warranted some research.

I got home, went online, and discovered that matadors can clear well over five hundred thousand dollars a year. A little more brows-ing turned up the San Diego–based California Academy of Tauro-maquia, which touted itself as America's only bullfighting academy. By the time Tara got home, I had a new plan. I told her that I had seen the job counselor and that he had been very helpful.

"I'm so happy," she said, wrapping her arms around me.

"He recommended I look into bullfighting," I said.

She dropped her arms and took a step back. At first, she thought I was joking. I assured her I wasn't.

"What kind of fucking job counselor did you go see? Is he a lunatic?"

I told her I'd seen Bob Fitch, and since she knew and liked the guy, she was momentarily stymied. It gave me a short reprieve to lay out my case.

"This is not crazy," I began. "I have a plan."

I explained that I was going to enroll in the California Academy of Tauromaquia for an accelerated weekend crash course in bull-fighting.

"A crash course in bullfighting?" she said, raising her eyebrows. "That sounds about right."

At the end of the weekend course, we could see if I had any skill. If I did, I'd head to Spain and try to join the bullfighting circuit for the last few weeks of the season. The capital investment was small. School fees were four hundred dollars, and a plane ticket to Spain was five hundred dollars. I figured the whole thing would weigh in at fifteen hundred dollars.

"And if I can get even one booking in Spain, I'll make a lot more than that," I told her. "That's pretty minimal risk."

"We're talking about fighting bulls," she retorted. "You're putting your testicles and our future children in harm's way. So don't talk to me about minimal risk."

She stared at me, trying to decide how to handle this.

"You are so difficult sometimes," she said, exasperated. "What's gotten into you? First armwrestling and now bullfighting? Why can't you just be a normal human being?"

I told her I didn't want to be a normal human being. In fact, I was convinced that everybody wants to be unique in some way. The people I admired—guys like Jeff Thomchesson and Rick Soliwada—had discovered what it was that differentiated them. Until I found whatever it was that made me unique, I was going to have to keep looking. And right now, it seemed to me that the bullring was calling my name.

"I think you need to see a shrink," Tara concluded. "And that's all I'm going to say for now."

Hank Berman's office was on the second floor of an old Victorian in Japantown. From his comfortable couch, I could see the trees on Fillmore Street. A box of Kleenex sat on the table beside me.

"Okay," Hank said, taking a breath mint out of a tin can. "What's going on? You want one of these? No? Why are you here?"

He had a New Yorker's bluntness, which I found comforting. I wanted to get through this as fast as possible. Tara said that she wouldn't let me bullfight unless I spoke to a therapist. A depressed friend of mine recommended Hank.

I wasn't happy to be there. I felt like I knew what I was doing but suddenly wondered if I really was a little unhinged. It was like being in a hospital when you're healthy—I felt sickness surrounding me, pushing in. Hank himself seemed mildly depressed, like he'd been sitting in this room too long. He rubbed his mostly bald pate, smoothed his graying mustache, and slumped in his frayed chair.

"My wife and I are having problems," I began. Hank nodded. He'd heard this before. But when I told him that she didn't want me to go fight bulls, he looked confused and waited for me to continue.

"That's it," I said. "She's losing faith in me."

"What exactly do you mean by bulls?" Hank said. "Is that a metaphor?"

"No, I want to be a bullfighter."

"I see." I could almost hear his cogitations: Schizophrenic? Delusional? Temporary mental breakdown?

"Listen, the reality is that I know I'm running out of time," I said. "I'm going to have to find a way of making a living, but I don't think that I'm that different from the next guy just because I'm trying to find a life that I actually think is worth living."

I told him that maybe I was taking it to a greater extreme, but because of my mom's prepping, I had started my search young. I'd been cycling through activities for decades, trying to find my greatest strength, or any strength, for that matter. So, from the outside it might look like I was doing crazy things, but that was only because I'd crossed all the noncrazy things off my list.

Hank stared at me impassively. I recognized the technique. When I interviewed people for my articles in the local weekly, I'd sometimes just look at them and stay silent. Usually, a conversation is filled with reassuring "uh-huhs" and other encouragements. Silence feels like an accusation, and the speaker usually interprets it as an accusation of whatever they feel most uncomfortable about. So even though I'd said nothing, I'd get quickly to the emotional center of the issue. I understood how this worked, but that didn't mean I was impervious to it.

"Okay, maybe it's a little unhealthy that my mom needs me to make up for her loss," I said, feeling the strain of his stare. "But that's really *her* issue. *My* motivations are personal now. I'm all grown up."

Those last words hung in the air and, with each passing second, sounded less and less convincing. Finally, Hank leaned forward.

"You know, in the sixties, there was a time when everyone was taking acid," he began. "I took it, it did some things to me. I remember that. But now I'm hearing you, and it reminds me of this Chinese proverb." For the next ten minutes, he told me an involved story about fishing and Chinese farmers. I had trouble following and was getting annoyed. I thought the acid memory might have short-circuited his brain.

"But all that is to say that I think you're fine," he suddenly concluded. "It's good what you're doing. We all need to figure out our potential."

The problem, he said, was answering the following question: Does everybody have unlimited potential or is that just a silly tale we tell kids in kindergarten? Because if there's a limit to our potential, then I have to figure out when I've met it and start settling for whatever I can get. Maybe, he said, that's what it means to grow up. You realize that your options narrow until there's only one possible path. The pragmatists of the world would argue it that way.

But the pragmatists could also be called losers, Hank said. Defeatists. Unhappy, lazy assholes. Because why would potential decrease as you got older and learned more? It's the opposite. Your potential increases as you get older. You're wiser, more capable, and more mature. People simply get complacent—it's not easy to keep challenging yourself—but without the challenge, life begins to lose its sparkle.

"So, like I said, none of this is the issue here with you," he said. "What I'm sensing is that you have trouble with compassion. You don't understand why your wife is upset with you. You can't feel what she's feeling."

It was true. I was overly focused on my own goals. To be honest, I didn't even know where Tara wanted to be in five years' time. I thought she was happy being a teacher but we had never really talked about it. I figured she would tell me if there was a problem. Hank shook his head when I said that. "Maybe you've gotten complacent in your marriage," he said. He told me that I should try asking her more questions, try to understand where she was in her life. Maybe there was untapped potential lurking below the surface of my marriage.

We had a quiet dinner at home that night, and when I asked, Tara told me that she wasn't happy being a teacher. It bothered her that teachers were not as respected as lawyers or doctors. When she first started teaching, she didn't care—she didn't need any external affirmation. But now she felt undervalued, overworked, and tired. She was burned-out.

I was surprised but stayed quiet and let her continue. She said she had been thinking of applying to law school. She could go into education law and try to help hundreds of thousands of students by strengthening California's education code. It would be valuable work and she would be respected.

It also meant that she was going to quit her job in six months and we'd have no income. It might have looked like my options were narrowing. But I felt invigorated. Both of our lives would now be in flux. It was scary and thrilling.

"And I think we should talk about having kids," she added.

Whoa.

"I'll be in school for three years," she said. "I'll have a flexible schedule. It'd be the perfect time."

She could see the panic in my eyes. I couldn't fathom having kids until I had completed this quest to figure myself out. Tara took my hand. "At least, let's go to a sperm bank in case your balls get ripped off in some bullring in Mexico."

A pert middle-aged woman greeted us in the reception area of the Sperm Bank of California in Berkeley. She had defiantly gray hair and an understanding demeanor. We sat down in her office and she fidgeted with a test tube.

"We have a lot of young clients such as yourselves who are busy professionals and just don't have time for sex anymore," she said. "They want to have children but are too busy for intimacy. So a combination of a turkey baster and the Sperm Bank of California does the trick."

"We actually have sex all the time," Tara said peevishly. She didn't like this woman.

"Oh, that's so good to hear," the lady said encouragingly, as if sex were a dying art. "Life is just so rushed nowadays. Intercourse is one of the first things people put aside."

Tara cut her short and, cunningly, told her we were in a rush. The lady frowned and directed us down a long hall toward a row of small "sample" rooms. A window at the end of the hall looked out on the International Language Studies Institute across the way. The window frame blocked out all the oversized, bold letters of the institute's sign except for STUD. Every patron of the sperm bank had to stare at those letters as he walked toward the sample rooms.

As Tara and I left the sperm bank, it struck me that I may well have just completed my contribution to the conception of our future child. If something happened to my testes in the ring, that moment at the sperm bank would be, for me, the moment of conception. In other words, I had just fathered a child. As opposed as I was earlier to the idea of having children, right now I felt a warm flush at the thought. This was no longer just about us supporting ourselves. I had to be responsible to the thousands of little sperm floating around in liquid nitrogen. I had to get serious.

I phoned the California Academy of Tauromaquia when I got home. Coleman Cooney, the academy's director, picked up. A baby was screaming in the background and a lady was yelling, "Shut up! Shut up! Shut up!"

"This is the California Academy of Tauromaquia. How can I help you?" Cooney said, raising his voice over the uproar.

I haltingly explained that I wanted to set up a private two-day session as soon as possible and Cooney invited me to come down the next weekend. He told me we'd spend Saturday going over the basics and then he'd put me in a Mexican bullring on Sunday, all for only four hundred dollars. All I needed to bring was tennis shoes.

I mentioned that I was a vegetarian and didn't want to hurt the bull. No poking or prodding. Just me and the bull—face-to-face. I wanted no unfair advantages. Cooney assured me that the bull would be happy to gore me if given half a chance. He added that we would be practicing the Portuguese-style bloodless bullfight—the matador simply performed passes with the bull and, if all went well, there was never contact between the two.

The next Friday, Tara and I got into our Buick and sped down to San Diego. Cooney had e-mailed me directions and we followed them to a large, newly completed middle-class housing development near the border with Mexico. Hundreds of identical three-bedroom homes lined the gently sloping streets in the fading afternoon light. All the trees were saplings and the roll-on grass in every front yard had yet to fully take to the new soil. A border-patrol helicopter hovered in the distance and periodically flashed a spotlight down onto the barren hills.

We parked in front of Cooney's house and he came out to greet us. He was a good-looking bald man in his mid-thirties and had a pretty wife, two small kids, and a sullen teenage stepson. All five of them were jammed into the house with two dogs, one of which was in heat and yelped continuously from an enclosed terrace.

Cooney motioned for us to sit on his couch and, without asking any questions, began his instruction while his five-year-old son played with a plastic bull on the carpeted floor. In the first few minutes, I learned that bullfighting was much more dangerous before penicillin was available and that 80 percent of bullfighting wounds occur in the groin area.

"I'll get a strap-on," I joked to Tara. She didn't think it was funny, particularly after Coleman said that there was at least one death every season.

"But bulls respond amazingly well to the signals I'm going to teach you," he said, speaking enthusiastically, like a motivational speaker. I implicitly believed him. Cooney had charisma. Despite the noise of his crying baby, the whining dog, and the interruptions of his five-year-old, I was captivated and listened closely to everything he said. Bob Fitch could have benefited from a talk with this guy.

Cooney listed a blur of specialized bullfighting terms: the *pase de pecho, veronicas, muleta, mozo de espadas.* It was as if he were introducing me to a secret society, a world that had its own language within a language. Finally, breathing heavily, he put in a videotape. Images of massive bulls chewing grass in Spain faded in on the TV. A narrator began talking in Spanish. I had no idea what he was saying. Cooney's son stood up and hurled the plastic bull at the wall. The bulls on TV kept munching.

"I know how to," the kid said, speaking over the Spanish narrator. "I know fight bulls."

"Oh, yeah?" I offered, trying to keep my eye on the TV for fear of missing an important clue into a bull's psyche. "What's the most important thing to know?"

"Don't move your feet," the kid said, jumping up and down on the plastic bull while Cooney got up to answer the phone.

"We have a slight change of plans," Cooney said when he hung up. "The *ganadero* at the ranch can only do it tomorrow, so we're going to have to get you ready real quick."

He pressed stop on the VCR (the bulls had moved to the shade beneath a tree) and we got back into the Buick. Ten minutes later, we were in a deserted parking lot and Cooney was running at me with his hands on his head, index fingers pointing up to indicate horns. He had given me a red cape, told me to keep it just in front of the "horns" as the "bull" passed and then lift the cape up.

The red cape, I now learned, was called the *muleta*. It was folded over a notched two-foot-long stick, which is what supported it. You held the stick through the cape's fabric and presented the target to the bull, making sure that the far end of the cape was angled slightly toward the animal. According to Cooney, the bull will instinctively attack the "leading edge"—the closest corner of the cape. If the end next to your body is angled toward the bull, the bull will follow that right into your thigh. But if the far end is closest to the bull, the animal will charge the outside of the cape and rush right past you.

Cooney explained that it had nothing to do with the color of the cape: red simply allowed the audience to better track the matador's movements. What mattered most was the angle of the cape, because that allowed the bullfighter to play off the animal's instincts.

"Now I'm going to give you two commands for tomorrow," Cooney concluded. "First is 'Run away!' That's pretty self-explanatory. Second is 'Go right at him.' That means walk directly toward the animal. If you're too far away, their instinct is to run away from you because you're not an immediate threat. But there is a line in every bull's mind. If you cross it, they attack. You have to find that line, so that's why I'll tell you to go right at him. Okay? I'll see you tomorrow at seven in the morning."

We slept at a Holiday Inn that night. Or, rather, Tara slept and I sweated. In the morning, my side of the bed was sticky, wet, and cold. Tara tried to convince me that I didn't have enough training. I told her that we hadn't come all this way to back out now.

We picked up Cooney and headed for the border in a slight drizzle. Cooney looked worried. He said that the dirt road to the bull ranch might flood if the rain picked up. Then he started rambling about the churchlike qualities of steak houses, his opinion that Israel should nuke the Palestinians, and misconceptions relating to naked bullfighting in pre-1940s cinema. By the time I got out of the car to buy Mexican car insurance, I realized that he was completely crazy.

Tara followed me in while Cooney waited with the car.

"I'm not getting back in that car," she said. "I can't believe you talked me into going to Mexico with a fucking nutcase."

I told her to just tune him out and convinced her that his skills as a bullfighting instructor were all that mattered. She doubted those as well but we got in the car, crossed the border, and drove west on a two-lane Mexican road somewhere between Tecate and Tijuana. The terrain became mountainous and was dotted with wet, green scrub brush and unpainted cinder-block homes. After half an hour of nonstop babble, Cooney interrupted himself to tell me to turn left onto an unmarked dirt road. He cautioned me to go slow. It was an unnecessary comment since a giant puddle barred the entrance to the road.

I eased the Buick into the water and we rolled steadily through it, like a baby-blue cruise liner. The water lapped up to the floorboard but didn't leak in. The road after that was strewn with boulders, water-filled ditches, and constant wash-board rutting. We drove at a crawl for about an hour into the wilderness before Cooney pointed to a white stucco wall and told us that we had arrived at the ranch.

The entrance was beautiful: old cottonwood trees lined a long road that ended in a collection of simple wooden farmhouses. The place looked like the real deal. There were even ranch hands waiting for us. When we got out, a deeply wrinkled old woman who appeared to be the groundskeeper approached me with a headless, writhing rattlesnake. She made eating motions and offered it to me. I rubbed my stomach to indicate that I was full.

Cooney shooed her away and motioned us into the back of a

nearby pickup truck. He spoke to the ranch hands in Spanish and kept saying the word *vaca*. Finally I asked him what it meant.

"It means 'cow,' " he said. "You're not ready for a bull just yet so we're going to put you in front of a smaller animal."

"I'm going to fight a cow?" I asked.

"Don't worry, it'll be scary. Trust me."

We headed out into the ranch's open pastures, which rested in a valley between thousand-foot mountains. Heavy cumulus clouds hovered above the mountaintops and threatened more rain. My heart started beating faster when we closed in on a herd of cattle foraging on the mountain's slope. I heard hoofbeats and looked over my shoulder to see a man on horseback gallop up alongside the truck. Cooney pointed at the herd and the cowboy spurred his horse toward them.

Within five minutes, the guy had chased the herd around in a semicircle, separated one small cow from the pack, lassoed it, and tied its legs together. Another two guys in a truck drove up the road, pulled up beside the downed cow, and hefted the three-hundred-pound animal into the back of their pickup.

All of us then drove back down the road and parked in front of a rustic but well-maintained bullring, complete with a thirty-person viewing stand. The ranch hands lifted the cow out of the truck, carried her over to a holding pen, and untied her. She sprang to her feet and aggressively swiveled her three-inch horns from side to side. Cooney was right: I was scared.

One of the ranch hands opened a thick metal door and I walked into the ring. It was about forty yards in diameter and had three *burladeros*—thick wooden barriers set in strategic locations on the perimeter. If a bullfighter gets into trouble, he can run behind one for protection. On the far side of the ring, a metal gate led to the *vaca*'s holding pen.

Cooney ran over the basic idea again ("run away" figured prominently), handed me a *muleta*, and wished me luck. He said that he would take a few passes with the *vaca* first to see if she had any abnormal instincts. He shouted out to the ranch hands, and in a second the metal gate rose with a thunderous clang.

Nothing happened.

"Hey, *vaca, vaca, vaca,*" Cooney called out, but the *vaca* didn't want to come.

One of the ranch hands leaned over the wall and waved his hands. He got a little closer and waved again. The *vaca* didn't budge. He moved a little closer and suddenly the animal lunged at him. He fell backward over the wall and landed loudly on the hard-packed earth outside while the *vaca* dashed into the bullring looking for something to kill. The metal gate smashed shut and the animal came to a suspicious halt in the middle of the ring.

Cooney edged out from behind the *burladero* and slowly approached the cow. He continually called out to it ("Hey, *vaca, vaca, vaca*"), and when he was within fifteen feet, he moved the *muleta* up and shook it. The *vaca* erupted, running full speed at him, and slammed right into him, totally ignoring the cape.

"She has some abnormal instincts," he shouted as he limped toward one of the *burladeros.* The cow's horns had sliced into the air on either side of him, miraculously missing his body. The *vaca* pawed and stomped on his *muleta,* which he had left behind in his haste to get away. "But if you come at her from the other direction, I think she'll be okay. Why don't you give it a try."

I glanced up at Tara. She was sitting in the viewing stands by herself, guzzling can after can of Mexican beer. She took another swig, waved at me, and shouted, "Go for it!" Her tone said, "I've got your sperm in a little vial back in Berkeley, so have all the fun you want."

When I do something nerve-racking, I usually feel like I'm watching myself from a safe distance. In this case, I felt myself walk out from behind the barrier and wondered if it was really me doing it. I think my mind was preparing itself for injury. It was trying to distance itself from the pain it expected my body to experience.

But when the *vaca* snorted at me, I snapped back to my senses. I realized that I was standing in a Mexican bullring in front of an angry animal nearly three times my weight. I registered that Cooney was shouting at me but I didn't care what he was saying. All of my attention was focused on the cow. I arched my back, slowly swung the *muleta* forward, and shouted, "*Vaca,* hey!"

The animal lunged toward me and I dragged the cape in front of its horns smoothly. The cow rushed past, her body no more than a few inches from my groin. I heard Tara drunkenly shout, "*Olé!*" And then, a second later, "Watch out!"

I looked over my shoulder in time to see that the cow had spun around with amazing agility and was bearing down on my right leg. I leaped into the air and landed on the animal's back. The cape slipped out of my hand but I slid off onto my feet and ran for the barrier. I made it just before the cow smashed its head into the wood.

"That looked very good," Cooney shouted. I couldn't tell if he was joking or not, but the rush of doing it right once tempted me back out into the ring. I wanted to do better.

One of the ranch hands sprinted into the ring and distracted the *vaca* while I ran out and picked up the two *muletas.* I gave Cooney his and for the next ten minutes performed a series of successful passes with the cow. Tara couldn't stop clapping and spilled most of her beer onto the viewing stands.

Eventually, the cow figured out that it wasn't getting anywhere and it just stopped charging. Cooney came out from behind the barrier and shook my hand.

"You've got natural talent," he said. "And we know you've got the balls because you made it here. You could be a good matador if you stick with it."

I had some big decisions to make when we got back to San Francisco. The obvious next step was to go to Spain but I didn't have any idea what I would do once I got there. There were surely schools and apprenticeships, but I didn't speak Spanish and I didn't know whom to contact. It seemed ridiculous and totally half-assed.

But then I asked myself, *What would Ipski-Pipski do?*

I called my editor at the local paper and told her I was changing careers. If Ipski-Pipski spotted something scary and overwhelming, he headed straight for it without thinking twice. I was far from the full embodiment of the ideal—I thought at least twice. Of course, my thinking wasn't very clear. Rather than keep my options open with the weekly, I told them, with a slight edge in my voice, that I was done writing strip club reviews. And yet before shutting down my computer, I sent off a Hail Mary pitch to *Wired* magazine. I figured writing wasn't for me if I had to evaluate menus at strip clubs. But if a national magazine let me write about something interesting, maybe I'd consider giving up bullfighting.

Wired didn't respond, and that path faded. From now on, I decided, I was going to be a bullfighter. I knew I was acting foolishly, but I tried to mitigate the madness by pursuing my new career in a realistic way. I admitted to myself that I couldn't make it on my own. I didn't have any contacts and would need someone who understood the European bullfighting scene. I decided to take out an ad in the local paper.

"Up and coming local bullfighter seeks manager to handle all aspects of operations. Travel the world and take home a percentage of the winnings."

It came out a week later and my phone wouldn't stop ringing. It seemed like everybody in San Francisco wanted to be my bullfighting manager. I got calls from firemen, circus managers, flamenco dancers, accountants, teachers, clerks, gas station attendants, and paralegals. I even got some propositions.

"My name is Gina and my nipples are hard like the horns of a bull," one syrupy voice whispered into my voice mail. "Call me. I want to *manage* you."

It took a few days but I found the perfect manager. Ironically, I already knew him. Carlos was the dean of students at Tara's high school, and when she mentioned my bullfighting obsession to him he said he was interested in the job.

Like Tara, Carlos wasn't satisfied with teaching or being an administrator. He had started as a Spanish teacher and got promoted to dean. He was the school's disciplinarian and spent his days with the jackasses who tried to smuggle booze into class or peed all over the bathroom. He was sick of his job and, miraculously, had an illustrious bullfighting background.

Carlos's grandfather, Manuel Roig, was a celebrated bullfighter in southern Spain in the forties and fifties. When Grandpa Roig hung up his cape, he managed Miguel Báez Litri, one of the world's best bullfighters in the 1990s. As a teenager, Carlos spent his summers in Spain working as the assistant manager. Carlos's dad wasn't interested in the business of bullfighting—he married an American and moved to California. But in Carlos, Grandpa Roig found an eager pupil, and happily mentored his grandson in the esoteric art of managing bullfighters.

But every fall, Carlos would return to California and go back to school like everyone else. He felt like he had a double life, and from the time he had graduated high school ten years ago, his life in America had dominated. He went to UC Berkeley, taught in a San Francisco public school, and was following a clearly defined track on the road to becoming a principal. But it just wasn't making him happy. When Tara mentioned I was looking for a bullfighting manager, it gave him goose bumps, as if a higher power were trying to make a point.

We met at a café for a perfunctory interview. We had chatted superficially in the past at high school social functions but had never discussed bullfighting. He had a lot of questions for me. If he was going to do this, it wasn't going to be some lark. He wanted to know how committed I was. I told him about Mexico, and the fact that I had already been in the ring impressed him. It was clear that I was willing to take the necessary risks.

We stared into our coffee mugs and Carlos sighed. He said this felt right to him. He was in his late twenties but his hair was already streaked with gray. If he was ever going to pursue his childhood dream of becoming a bullfighting manager, now was the time. I told him that if he wanted to manage my bullfighting career, I was willing to offer him a fifty-fifty split on the take. I stuck out my hand and we shook on it.

We bought tickets to Spain that weekend and Carlos called his grandfather. The old matador lived in a southern Spanish seaside town called Punta Umbria and, according to Carlos, spent his days smoking cigars and watching bullfights on TV. The plan was for us to fly into Madrid, train down to Punta, ask the patriarch's advice, and take it from there.

Saying goodbye to Tara was hard. She was concerned about my safety but I kept reminding her that Cooney had said I had talent. If I could place seventeenth in the world as an armwrestler with no skill whatsoever, imagine what I could do in a field where I was actually talented. I was going to do right by her and the children we already had in deep freeze in Berkeley.

The high-speed train rocketed us out of Madrid and into the Spanish countryside. We passed crumbling castles, giant posters of bulls (which were actually wine ads), and faded terra-cotta-tiled villages. It was an easy four-and-a-half-hour ride to the ocean, and Carlos's granddad was waiting for us on the platform when we arrived.

Though a little stooped at eighty-one, Manuel Roig was still a dashing figure. He wore well-tailored shirts, sunglasses, and had slicked-back gray hair. When he saw us, he threw away the butt of a cigar to kiss Carlos on both cheeks, shook my hand with both of his, and welcomed us to *"la buena vida."*

A short, muscley man stood beaming beside Grandpa Roig, and after Carlos kissed the man on the cheeks, he introduced me. This was Alin, a close family friend and the *mozo de espadas* (literally, "boy of the swords," but right-hand man is a better translation) of

Litri, the famed bullfighter. Alin looked me up and down and said something in Spanish.

"He says you have the body of a bullfighter," Carlos translated.

Over lunch and three bottles of Spanish wine, Carlos slowly revealed our plan to Alin and his granddad. We ate at Grandpa Roig's apartment in a high-rise building overlooking the Atlantic. The apartment was cramped. Carlos and I would have to share a small room with a bunk bed, but the view was fantastic. We were out on a spit, jutting into the ocean. On the mainland across the water, we could see the soaring white tower of La Rábida, the Franciscan monastery where Columbus set sail for the New World. The nearest big town, Huelva, was fifteen miles inland.

The lunch was made up of bread and whole shrimp. We had to pull the heads off and peel back the shells. It took forever and I made a mess while Carlos talked. When he got to the part about how I was going to make money as a matador, both of the Spaniards started laughing.

They talked to Carlos for a while, and then he explained to me that, first of all, you can't just say you're a matador. There is a long apprenticeship and you have to be sponsored by another matador. It's like a club. Second, only the top matadors make money. Unless you're in the top ten, you probably have to have a day job.

Carlos said that these were obviously problems but that there were some back doors we could use. The first option was to become an *espontáneo*—a spontaneous one. This route requires you to buy a front-row seat at a bullfight and sneak in a *muleta* under your shirt. When the matador in the ring takes a break between passes, the *espontáneo* leaps into the ring, whips out his *muleta*, and tries to astound the audience with his bullfighting prowess.

This method has typically been the recourse of impoverished bullfighters who don't have the money to sustain themselves as apprentices for multiple years. A good example occurred in Huelva a few months earlier. A young Japanese man named Taira Nono had seen a television program about matadors in Tokyo and decided to devote his life to becoming a bullfighter. He broke up with his girl-friend, bought a plane ticket to Madrid, and arrived in Spain. He had about a hundred euros in his pocket.

The first thing he did was buy a bullfighting magazine. He discovered that the next scheduled bullfight would take place in Huelva, a town he had never heard of. Like me, he spoke no Spanish, but he didn't even have a manager. He took the train to Huelva, watched the fight, and started showing up every morning at the ring where the matadors trained.

Huelva is a town of 150,000 people. It feels even smaller and attracts almost no tourists. The bullring, the most prominent landmark, is hidden in a labyrinth of narrow one-way streets near the middle of town. It's painted yellow and looks grand and old, but Seville's ring, about sixty miles away, eclipses it entirely. Nobody goes to Huelva, but Nono did, and out of curiosity the matadors at the ring invited him in and started to teach him. Eventually, they got him a job picking oranges, and for two years Nono became an orange picker in the early morning and a budding matador for the rest of the day.

But he knew that he was never going to have enough money to buy real bulls to practice with. Nor would he ever be able to afford a two-thousand-dollar bullfighting outfit. So, three months before I arrived, Nono leaped over the wall during a fight. He was wearing jeans and a T-shirt and caught the two-thousand-odd spectators completely by surprise. There had only been one Japanese matador and he was killed in the ring last season. To many, Nono looked like an apparition—the Japanese matador back from the dead to settle a score with the bulls.

Nono strode out and, to the horror of the crowd, lowered himself to his knees in front of the twelve-hundred-pound bull. It was the first animal he had ever been in front of and he was performing a matador's single most daring move. Theoretically, the bullfighter is supposed to kneel and swing his cape off to one side as the beast charges, fooling the animal into charging by his side. There is no room for error—if he does it wrong, the bullfighter gets gored in the face and most likely dies.

Nono had a lot of things going against him. He was Japanese, didn't speak Spanish, and didn't come from a bullfighting family. He knew that he had one shot at making it before the cops hauled him off to jail for disrupting the fight and he needed to make as big an impression as he could. He had decided to risk everything.

When the bull charged, Nono swung the cape perfectly and the beast charged past him. He swiveled and called the animal back. Again, Nono spun the cape like an expert and the crowd melted. They cried *"Olé!"* and *"Viva El Japonés!"* When the cops moved into the ring to grab him, there was such an uproar of boos and hisses that they retreated and Nono continued to perform brilliant passes. Finally, he blew kisses to the crowd (who gave him a standing ovation) and turned himself in to the authorities.

But the plaza owner refused to press charges. In fact, he did just the opposite. He offered Nono a three-fight contract. El Japonés had made his dream come true by stepping out as an *espontáneo.*

I, however, was in a slightly different position. Nono had trained for two years. I had trained for two days. Alin and Grandpa Roig insisted that I would be killed if I tried to fight a twelve-hundred-pound bull. But there was a second option. In addition to the main bullfighting circuit, there was a secondary tour, kind of like the minor leagues. It was called "El Bombero Torero."

When Grandpa said it, Alin burst out laughing and Carlos immediately said no. I asked him what it was but he was too busy denouncing the idea in Spanish to tell me. Finally, he explained that the term meant "fireman bullfighter." It's a bullfight where a bunch of midgets come out in a fire truck and try to run circles around the bull. Then one of the midgets dresses up in a miniature matador outfit and performs a series of passes.

"Abuelo thinks that they might be interested in a vegetarian, Californian bullfighter," Carlos said, sounding less peeved. "And he does have a point: the bulls are smaller."

For me, this was not about pride. It was about making a living, and I would do what I had to do to make it work. If the midgets provided the right audience for me, then so be it. Carlos opened the newspaper and found that the Bomberos were going to be in a town three hours away the following day. We decided to borrow the family car and offer my services.

Grandpa toasted the decision—we'd finished three bottles of wine and now he thought it was a good idea for me to join the midgets. Alin stood up, wobbled for a second, and announced that we had to leave with him immediately. He needed to give me something before we left so we drove ten minutes to his house. It was a big, recently built home done up with stucco to make it look old. Inside, the walls were lined with photos of Alin posing beside bullfighters. There were at least a dozen garish oil paintings of bulls in fields, bulls and matadors, bulls and horses, and bulls on the beach.

Alin led us up a narrow staircase to a thick wooden attic door, which was secured with two deadbolts. He took a key ring jammed with keys out of his pocket, unlocked the door, and motioned us through. Inside, hanging from the rafters like a hidden treasure, there were at least sixty *trajes de luces*, the "suit of lights," which a matador wears in the ring. Each one was fantastically embroidered with gold and silk. It looked like the dressing room of a king in hiding.

Alin explained that they all belonged to Litri, but since Litri had retired two years ago, they were of no use to anyone until now. Alin told me that even if I was working with midgets I would need an outfit, and he wanted to give me one. Carlos was certainly following an untraditional management path, but Alin still wanted to help his friend and younger colleague. Plus, he could sense our enthusiasm, and since Litri's retirement things had been a little quiet. Our arrival gave Alin something to get excited about.

He flipped through the suits until he found one he liked and handed it to me. It was white with black embroidery and was clearly a very expensive outfit. I told him it was too much, too generous. He insisted and Carlos advised me to take it.

"We don't have enough money to buy one and he'll take it as an insult if you refuse," he said. "And, just so you know, that's a Fermin suit. It doesn't get any better than that."

But accepting it was not the problem—putting the thing on proved to be a major production. First, there was the white leotard, then pink stockings, followed by pants so tight that Alin recommended I position my testicles to one side or risk having them bisected. The outfit is too difficult to put on solo: every matador needs someone to help him dress. In my case, Alin had to lift me off the ground and shake me into the pants to get them on.

I remembered when I put on the Team USA jacket for the first time in Poland and how it made me feel like I belonged. This took me a step further. The suit fit perfectly, which was amazing for a skintight outfit. I walked around the room with my chest puffed up, my back arched. Alin said it was a sign from God: there weren't many people who could wear Litri's suit. It was as if it had been tailored for me. I was made to be a bullfighter, Alin said.

The next morning, Carlos and I set out in the family Volvo with the suit of lights hanging in the backseat. We drove through the rolling hills and rocky outcroppings of the Andalusian countryside and into an old Moorish fortress town called Arcos de la Frontera. The town's aging fortress walls rose up precariously along a steep, crumbling cliff, which supported, at its apex, a hauntingly dark and damaged medieval church. We knew we were in the right place when we saw midgets on miniature motorcycles zooming through the cobblestone streets screaming, "Bombero Torero!" and honking their high-pitched horns.

Carlos and I parked and zeroed in on the bullring, which was in a field on the edge of town. The ring was collapsible and had probably been trucked in for the event. It was also very small and couldn't seat more than five hundred. Still, it was a bullring, which was better than nothing.

Carlos made some inquiries and within half an hour we were stooping underneath the folding bleachers with Pepito, the lead midget, who was in the process of putting on a shrunken suit of lights. I tried not to stare, but it was hard. Pepito, obviously not shy, stripped down to his underwear. He was in his late thirties and had probably gotten used to people staring at him.

Carlos explained who I was in Spanish and Pepito craned his neck to get a good look at me. Spanish audiences, Carlos said, would be amused by an American bullfighter, particularly since I wasn't very good yet and would probably get hit a lot. Considering the recent anti-American sentiment stemming from the imminent war in Iraq,

Carlos Roig

it might serve a cathartic purpose for the audience. Since I wasn't following the Spanish, I just nodded and smiled.

Carlos stopped talking and Pepito looked back and forth between the two of us before saying something curt to Carlos.

"He says you're not a midget," Carlos translated, sounding defeated.

"We know that," I said. "We've known that for a long time. What I'm offering is something he doesn't have. Ask him how many vegetarian, Californian bullfighters he has in his repertoire. Ask him that."

Carlos duly translated and Pepito responded.

"He's still having a problem with the fact that you're not a midget," Carlos said.

"I'll fight on my knees."

Pepito spoke for a minute and then stuck out his hand. We both shook it and he waddled away. I looked at Carlos.

"He says that people come to see Bombero Torero because they like to see midgets. You're not a midget, so it's pretty much dead on arrival."

The drive home was quiet and tense.

"Something's gonna happen," Carlos said. "Don't worry about it."

But I was worried. I fidgeted in the car until Carlos snapped at me because I was tapping my fingers on the door handle. I stopped for a minute and then started again. I was angry with him for not doing a better job of trying to convince the midgets. He was the manager, after all. I was just the talent. He was supposed to get me the gigs. He should have been *making* something happen.

When we got back to his grandfather's place late that night, Carlos had rebounded and come up with a new idea.

"We're going to put together our own fight," he said with hushed enthusiasm from the top bunk. "We'll have a poster made, we'll rent a ring for an afternoon, advertise the hell out of it, and we'll make a killing. What do you think?"

"Where do we get the bulls?" I said.

"I'll talk to my grandfather about that."

Over breakfast the next morning, Grandpa Roig assured us that he could get us both a ring and a bull for free. He doubted anyone would show up, but that was our problem. It wasn't going to be a big, famous ring. He said he had a friend with a place out in the countryside. All we needed to do was advertise effectively.

Carlos made a few calls to printers and found out that it was going to be prohibitively expensive to print a poster. First you had to hire an artist to draw it, and then the offset printing costs were a minimum of five hundred euros. We didn't have that kind of money, forcing Carlos to come up with another idea.

We took a day trip to Seville and scanned the tourist shops near the bullring. One hawker was selling generic, blank bullfight posters. The gimmick was that, for an extra ten bucks, he'd ink your name onto the poster with a set of cheap letter stamps. The sample hanging in the window was all we needed to see. Three quarters of it depicted the classic painted young bullfighter mid-pass with a bull. The bottom said, "Your Name Here."

The shop was crowded with Andalusian postcards, ashtrays, shot glasses, teaspoons, and ceramic dolls. Ahmed, the Moroccan storekeeper, looked like he had just popped a handful of Vicodin. He had big dark bags under his eyes and was about ready to fall asleep. A cigarette dangled from his mouth, sending up a thin line of smoke. He said it would cost about twenty euros to do a complete poster. Carlos looked at me and said we had some decisions to make.

First, what was my bullfighting name? Everybody had a bullfighting name. Taira was "El Japonés." Miguel Báez Litri was simply "Litri." The top bullfighter in the world, Julian Lopez, was "El Juli." I had to decide what I wanted to be called.

The second issue was that I couldn't be on the poster by myself. Usually, there were three matadors on a single billing, though sometimes they did a mano a mano with just two. We decided to put Carlos in the second slot and then just tell the audience that he fell ill.

The first problem was a little harder to crack. We needed something that would grab people's attention and indicate that this was going to be a spectacle, something they had never seen before. I offered "Don Joshua de Ranchero San Francisco," but Carlos said it didn't resonate. He preferred "El Sin Esperanza"—The One with No Hope. He thought audiences would come to see me get slaughtered. I was okay with that if it sold tickets, but the title didn't say anything about me being American.

That's when Carlos came up with "El Americano Desesperado"—The Desperate American. It said everything. And Carlos would be "El Apoderado Desesperado"—The Desperate Manager.

We went back in and laid it on Ahmed. Groggily, he told us that he couldn't do it. His stamp collection could only fit twelve characters horizontally on the poster. After ten minutes of wrangling, Carlos convinced him to just sell us a blank poster. We'd figure out how to ink it ourselves.

We went down the street to a Chinese restaurant for lunch and laid the poster on the table.

"What are we going to do with just one poster?" I asked.

"We'll leave it up in each place for a little while before moving it."

"We're going to have one poster and move it from place to place?"

"Listen, something's gonna happen," Carlos said, repeating his new favorite line.

I tried to get him to be a little more specific but he was distracted by the sight of a Chinese guy painting a mountainous landscape on the wall beside the kitchen door. "Hold on one second."

Carlos got up, walked over to the guy, and introduced himself. He pointed in my direction, and after a minute the two of them walked back to our table.

"This is Mr. Fa," Carlos said. "Mr. Fa is a very accomplished painter and he says that he's an expert in calligraphy, so I've asked him if he would do us the honor of penning our names on the poster."

He patted Fa on the back and the man smiled uneasily. Fa was clearly having a hard time understanding Carlos. Carlos didn't seem to notice. He whipped out his notepad and wrote out our names and monikers. He fished out a twenty-euro note from his pocket, handed it to the guy, unrolled the poster, and pointed at the blank area.

"Those letters go right here," Carlos said. "Do you think you can do it?"

The man looked at the names, looked at the poster, and put the money in his pocket. He nodded his head. *"Sí,"* he said with a thick Chinese accent. *"Dos horas."*

We finished eating, went for a stroll, and came back two hours later. Fa nodded at us, solemnly led us to a table near the back, and unrolled the poster. The blank area was filled in with beautiful hand-painted Chinese lettering. He had translated our names into Mandarin.

"For Christ's sake," Carlos moaned. But then, recovering quickly, he smiled and shook Fa's hand. "It's wonderful. Thank you so much."

We walked out with the poster. "This is a blessing in disguise," Carlos said.

"How do you figure that?" I snapped.

He said that we could easily make our own letters and tape them over the Chinese. Then we'd have a dual-purpose poster, one that could speak to two distinct populations. He said that the Chinese in Spain had historically been overlooked when it came to bullfight advertising. There was untapped potential there. Just the fact that we were speaking to them in their own language would interest them and make them feel welcome.

"Nobody's ever marketed a bullfight to the Chinese," Carlos said.

"Maybe there's a reason," I fired back.

"Yeah, it's called discrimination."

"No, Carlos, it's called the Chinese don't give a shit about bullfighting," I said.

"Something's gonna happen, okay?"

"Goddamnit, stop saying that."

I told him that the whole thing was a disaster. His managing skills needed some serious work. He in turn told me that if he was a bad manager, then I was a horrendously bad matador. We started yelling at each other in front of the Chinese restaurant. Spaniards coming home from work gave us a wide berth.

"Listen!" Carlos shouted finally. "It's not going to do us any good to scream at each other, okay? We can either give up or keep trying. It's that simple."

We stood in silence for a minute looking at each other. He was right. There were only two options and neither of us wanted to give up. Going home without even so much as a poster would be a terrible failure.

We walked until we found a stationery store and bought a stencil set, masking tape, a black marker, and thick red paper. Carlos got a table at a bar next door, ordered two beers, and we started coloring in the letters on the paper. Eventually, we patched together an unusual but legible marquee.

"It'll definitely attract attention," I said in a conciliatory tone.

Carlos went to a pay phone outside, called his grandfather, and came back glowing.

He penned another set of letters and taped them to the top part of the poster: LA PLAZA DE TOROS DE CABEZILLA PELADA — MEDIODÍA — 1 OCTUBRE.

"That's where we're doing it?" I asked.

"The Bald Head Bullring," Carlos said. "That's us. Abuelo's got you scheduled for an intensive week of training at the plaza in Huelva and that'll give me time to position this poster around town. So it's on. I told you something was going to happen."

El Profesor, the head instructor at the Huelva bullring, was a man in his late forties who was otherwise known as Miguel. Though the vertical creases of his face matched the perfect pleats in his pants, he had the strut of a young, arrogant man. When Alin dropped me off, El Profesor grunted at me, disappeared into a shed underneath the stands, and came back with a soccer ball. With a peevish wave, he indicated that I should follow him into the ring.

Walking through the bull gates and into a proper ring for the first time sent shivers through me. It was enormous—the ring was 120 feet across and the stands rose up like mountains on all sides. It felt surprisingly intimate, almost claustrophobic. There were no corners to hide in. The ground of the ring itself was yellowish, sandy dirt, which sloped up to the center in a slight hill. Standing in the middle was like standing on a small mountain in the Himalayas. Even at this highest point in the ring, I was lower than the lowest row of seats. The dirt and the ring's arched entrances made me feel like a gladiator in ancient Rome. In modern sports, there are no true rings anymore. There are a lot of ovals, and a boxing ring is square. But bullfights occur in a perfect circle and there's a power in that. It has a ceremonial feel that other sports facilities lack. It suggests that what goes on here is more than just spectacle.

El Profesor tossed the soccer ball into the middle of the ring and shouted. There were eight other students lounging around the perimeter, talking in small groups and smoking cigarettes. As the ball rolled into the center of the ring, they lazily followed it. Most were in their early twenties, though a few looked older. There was one Japanese guy—I found out later that this was Nono.

Before I fully processed what was happening, I had been assigned a team and we were playing soccer. Two *burladeros*—roughly opposite each other—served as goals. Periodically, the ball got kicked into the stands and someone had to climb the wall that Nono had famously jumped. We played for about an hour and then everyone shook hands and went home. There was no instruction, no talk of bulls. Just soccer.

The next day, the same thing happened. El Profesor threw the ball into the middle, we split up into teams, and we played another hour of soccer. This was not my idea of intensive bullfighting training. I understood that matadors needed to be in good shape, but a well-trained matador shouldn't have to run. If anything, he should be standing in place for an hour. That would do him more good.

There was another hour of soccer on the third day, but at the end of the hour I took matters into my own hands and put myself in front of El Profesor.

"*Yo quero torear,*" I said, summoning my best Taco Bell Spanish. I want to bullfight.

"*Si!*" he said, looking at me for the first time. "*Bueno.*"

He shouted at one of the younger students and the guy disappeared under the stands. A second later, he came out rolling a five-feet-tall fiberglass bull on wheels.

El Profesor tossed me a *muleta*, jutted his chin in my direction, and motioned for the student to attack with the bull. The guy leaned forward and essentially disappeared behind the hulking fiberglass bull, which started rolling quickly toward me. I set up as best I could.

"No, no, no!" El Profesor screamed, bringing the bull to a halt before me. He stormed over and started pushing my arms around as if I were one of those poseable wooden dolls that artists use. He spoke rapidly in a steady stream of Spanish that was clearly meant to be belittling.

I wasn't getting whatever it was he wanted to show me, so he pushed me aside in disgust and demonstrated. The student rolled the bull toward him and he executed a few fluid passes. He thrust the *muleta* back at me, and, to his surprise, I mimicked his movements almost perfectly when the student ran the fiberglass bull past me.

"*Bueno,*" he said, clapping his hands. Then he took back the *muleta* and walked away.

The next day we started with an hour's worth of soccer, but when the game ended, El Profesor had the student bring out the fake bull again. This time we stood in the middle of the ring and the professor didn't push my arms around quite as much.

"*Mas delicato,*" he said over and over, pointing at the way I was holding the *muleta.* *"Es como la espalda de una mujer"*—it's like a woman's back.

He taught me a sequence of passes that linked up beautifully together, ending with a *pase de pecho,* a movement at the end of the series where you release the bull from your control and walk away with your back turned. I had seen it performed while watching TV with Carlos's grandfather and had wanted to learn it.

Miguel taught me until the other student refused to run the bull any longer. As we walked out, he slapped me on the back.

"No malo," he said. Not bad.

It was hard to focus when I arrived at our venue for the big day. I was concerned both that I wouldn't perform well and that it wouldn't matter either way because no one would show up. I wasn't encouraged by the fact that the ring was three miles down an unmarked, partially flooded dirt road. Carlos strung balloons on a fence post at the cutoff on the main road, but he didn't have any helium so they sagged toward the ground.

He was confident, though. He had spent the week moving our Chinese-Spanish poster from location to location around Andalusia, sometimes hitting as many as fifteen spots a day.

"It's all about eyes," he said. "Every set of eyes that passed over that poster registered it. Maybe they didn't stop, but it worked on them subconsciously."

I had my doubts but I kept them to myself. I had a job to do. I was the main attraction—the only attraction, in fact—and I needed to be in top form to fight the bulls.

The ring was beautiful but small. It was smaller even than the one I had first fought at in Mexico. The stands could only accommodate about twenty people. Carlos assured me that it could hold more but told me that he was going to raise the ticket price from twenty to thirty euros. Regular fights usually cost much more, he said, so people would be comfortable with this.

Of course, Carlos was assuming that someone would show up. We were definitely in the countryside: I couldn't see another building in any direction. There were only rolling hills, wild olive trees, and dusty oaks. The ring was built from stone and covered with smooth white stucco. There were no sounds other than our voices: no cars, no buses, not even an airplane overhead. It was as if we'd traveled back to the nineteenth century, when fighting with animals in a ring was a normal, even vital, activity. It was a time when man lived in proximity to animals and needed to assert his dominion.

Now, as part of a generation raised indoors and on the Internet, why was I so attracted to being in the ring? What impact could it have on a life lived online in a big city (other than an intensely painful, physical kind of impact)? Sure, I hoped I could generate some income from it but, honestly, that was looking less and less likely as the stands remained empty and Carlos paced nervously in the gravel parking lot. So why go through with it?

Ipski-Pipski wouldn't have hung up his cape and gone home in the face of defeat. For better or for worse, this was my job now. Just because no one showed up, it didn't mean that I wasn't a bullfighter. I was a professional and I was going to do my job with all the passion in me, audience or no audience.

"Something's gonna happen," Carlos commented, furrowing up his brow. "Everything's going to be okay."

I nodded somberly, shook his hand, told him I hoped he was right, and walked back into the changing area, where Alin helped me suit up. I did hear at least one car arrive, which perked me up a little. When I was ready, Alin crossed himself and led me into the ring. I followed, trying to look as regal as possible.

Not including Carlos, there were two people in the stands, but I didn't have time to contemplate that. The ranch hands jerked the bull gate open and Alin pulled me back behind a *burladero*. A pissed-off five-hundred-pound bull ran out. It had short curled horns and jerked its head back and forth, ready to pummel the first thing it set its eyes on. It snorted its rage.

"Be careful," Alin cautioned, and patted me on the back.

To be honest, the bull was scaring the hell out of me. It dashed at our *burladero* and tried to angle its horns in at me. It tore a chunk out of the barrier before racing off to the other side of the ring. I took a deep breath and stepped out from behind the blockade. I was free game now. Nothing stood between the animal and me.

"Hey, *toro, toro, toro*," I said, so quietly that I could barely hear it myself. The bull was facing away from me and was pawing at the ground in front of the wall.

Okay, I said to myself, *this is it. You've trained for this. You know what to do. You've got to calm down and focus. You have no choice but to focus. You have a family to support.*

I arched my back a little more, stuck out my chin, and shouted, "HEY, *TORO*!"

The bull swung around with a grunt. I slowly brought the *muleta* forward and shook it while flicking the hair out of my face with a toss of my head. I suddenly felt calm. I felt like I knew what I was doing.

The bull eyed the *muleta* with suspicion and then charged. I kept the cape steady, with the outside edge angled forward. The bull went for it and I dragged the cape around my body, leading the animal in a circle around me. When my right arm was fully extended and I was looking back over my shoulder, I spun around in one smooth movement and brought the bull toward me again. I spun a second time and brought him even closer. The ground shook with the impact of his hooves. I could hear him breathing. We were dancing: I was leading, he was following. We were completely in sync with each other.

On the fourth charge, I swirled the *muleta* into my left hand at the end of the pass. The red cloth rippled liked a butterfly flapping its wings. The bull turned around to follow it and waited for my next move. With an almost imperceptible shake of my hand, he drove toward the cape again. This time I raised it high as he passed, causing him to rear his head up and run straight away from me. I pivoted, facing my back to him, and walked calmly away. I had performed the classic *pase de pecho*.

For an audience of two, they sure sounded loud. Their cheers resounded like those of at least ten people. With each subsequent pass, they shouted, *"Olé!"* and clapped. But after another series of passes, the bull gave up and lay down. It was still young and didn't have the strength to keep running. Alin told me to let it rest and Carlos shouted for me to come up and meet the audience.

The audience was my friend Cristian Sessa and his Mexican girlfriend. Cristian was an Argentinean film producer who was in Spain for the San Sebastián Film Festival. I had sent him an e-mail telling him to come see my performance and he made arrangements to get here.

It was a bittersweet pleasure to see him. It meant that no one independently showed up to our bullfight. Cristian magnanimously paid us sixty euros but we were still depressed. It wasn't what we had hoped for.

The next bull was even smaller. In fact, *bull* is too grand a term for this animal. First, it wasn't a bull, it was a *vaca*—a cow. Second, it didn't weigh more than two hundred pounds and had little nubbins for horns. It was a baby cow, but it responded beautifully to my *muleta.* The dance made me forget my failure. I was good at this, even if I hadn't made any money and had no prospects. The baby cow and I swiveled around each other, playing off the combined fear and instinct in both of us. I wasn't thinking about what I was doing; my body was moving confidently.

I'm sure it looked ridiculous: a grown man and a small cow bound together in a remote bullring in southern Spain. She was a puny, skinny creature and, even though I'm skinny and puny, too, I towered over her. She must have been scared, but as soon as she saw me from across the ring she started running toward me. She wasn't intimidated—in fact, she was sure she was going to kick my ass. For my part, I felt a startling surge of discovery. I wasn't sure that I was going to kick her ass, but I was exuberantly curious to see what would happen. The intensity of the experience forced me to realize what was at my core: an unbridled, unstoppable curiosity. I didn't need answers. I was addicted to questions.

But I knew that whether this little animal would gore me in the shin was one of the last questions I would get to answer. It seemed a shame that as soon as I discovered something, I would have to bury it. When the cow and I finally exhausted each other, she would go back to her fenced-in field and I would go home and get an office job.

I called Tara that night from Grandpa Roig's to tell her I was giving up. I'd look for a regular job—maybe in an ad agency—and take a temp position back in data entry in the meantime. Tara interrupted me to say that there was a message on our voice mail from *Wired*, the magazine I had pitched when I got back from Mexico. The editor said he wanted to commission the article. He was offering me real money to go out into the world and ask questions.

"Are you kidding?" I asked.

"No, baby," she said sweetly. "You did it."

I shouted *"Olé!"* so loud, she had to hold the phone away from her ear.

"Olé?" Grandpa Roig asked, startled by my sudden outburst in his kitchen.

I had my first national writing assignment.

Joshua Davis Collection

CHAPTER THREE

BEING
BIG

When I got back from Spain, I threw myself whole-heartedly into that first feature for *Wired*. It was an article about Amish farmers who were growing genetically modified, nicotine-free tobacco. The questions made me drool—they were so exciting, it felt sexual.

Because of what I had learned in the bullring, I let my curiosity take me wherever it saw fit. Before the war in Iraq began, I convinced *Wired* to send me as their war correspondent. The questions led me to dangerous places but were captivating enough to keep the fear at bay, just like they did when I was fighting bulls.

When I got back from Iraq, *Wired* made me a contributing editor. They put me on staff and began sending me a check every month. I wasn't a champion in anything but I felt like I had won something. Tara and I were able to move to a slightly larger apartment that fulfilled most of her demands. It had good light and enough room to leave the dining table permanently set up. The only thing missing was a bathtub so we still had that to aspire to. But she was happy and that made me happy. She quit her job and started law school.

For the rest of the year, I pursued stories in Singapore, Kathmandu, Jerusalem, London, and Antwerp. I asked a lot of questions but there was one I constantly avoided. Tara wanted to know when we were going to have kids and I didn't have an answer for her. I knew I wasn't ready and I also didn't want to disturb the life we were building. I didn't want to have to compromise to make room for babies. I enjoyed traveling at a moment's notice, having quiet nights at home, and being able to do whatever we wanted. Basically, I was too selfish to have kids.

In the abstract, I liked the concept of fatherhood, but only insofar as I could pick and choose when I wanted to be a father. Unfortunately, I was pretty sure it wasn't going to work out that way. Tara had already put me on notice that when it did happen, I was going to be changing a lot of diapers and staying up late to rock the kid to sleep. Just the thought of it exhausted me.

And yet it was going to happen at some point. It wasn't like Tara was going to give up on the idea, but I couldn't figure out what I needed to do to get ready. I guess a lot of people just have kids and then deal with it, but that didn't seem ideal. It was too big a decision to stumble into, and in many ways I still felt like a kid myself. Basically, I needed to grow up a little more.

The question was, how could I make myself grow up on pace with Tara's biological clock? To answer that, I needed to first figure out what my issues were. Since my parents split up when I was three and my mom remarried when I was ten, I had two examples of fatherhood to judge myself by and determine where I came up lacking. My real dad is six feet four inches, has a significant potbelly, and, at times, a big white-man's afro. My stepdad, John, on the other hand, still wears his hair close to the crew cut he had in Vietnam. He is six feet two inches, two hundred pounds, and solidly built, a natural athlete. Before he was drafted, he water-skied one hundred miles nonstop from the Pacific Ocean to Portland, Oregon, just for fun.

After he married my mom, he gave me his medals from Vietnam, and even those seemed oversized in my hands.

So the one thing I knew for sure was that a dad was someone big.

And, at five feet eight inches and 128 pounds, I was not big.

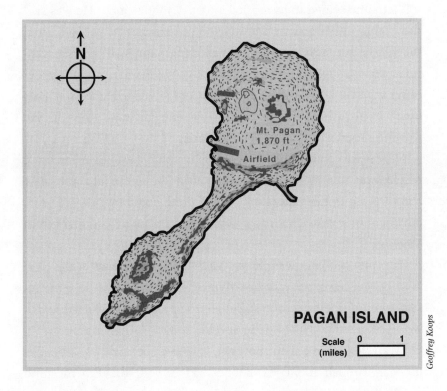

PAGAN ISLAND

Scale (miles) 0 1

Geoffrey Koops

My mom called and told me that John wanted to get into the sardine business. A couple of years ago, they had left the San Francisco Bay Area to move to Astoria, the small fishing town in northern Oregon where John grew up. Rumors were now swirling about the first major sardine run since 1941.

"You know the Japanese love sardines, right?" Mom said.

"No, I didn't know that."

"Well, they do. And John has this great idea."

John was an entrepreneur whose last major venture was to buy the mining rights to an active volcano in the South Pacific. Unfortunately, it was very difficult to do any mining because the volcano kept blowing up. John still kept an impressively large map of the island hanging behind his desk, but it didn't reassure investors. First, the island was named Pagan. Second, it was shaped like a flaccid penis.

Vietnam seemed to have fried a part of John's brain. He was still the affable, sweet man he'd always been, but when he got back from the war he set off on a series of increasingly unusual business ventures. He tried to pave a freeway through the Sri Lankan jungle, became the sole U.S. licensee for miniature silver wildebeest statues made in Africa, and attempted to establish a new town in the Kuwaiti desert. Each failed spectacularly.

Now it was pickled fish. According to the fisherman at the diner where John ate lunch, sardines were abandoning the Japanese coast and thriving in the waters off Oregon. John could buy them cheap, put them in a jar with vinegar, and sell them for a good markup in Tokyo.

The only problem was that he didn't know anybody in the fish-distribution business in Japan. My mom wanted me to do some research online. "He needs to start meeting people in the Japanese fish world," she said. "He needs to develop some relationships."

"Well, let's think about how the Japanese socialize," I said, talking her through it on the phone. "They golf, they go to sumo matches, they sing karaoke."

I did a little research online while we were talking and found the California Sumo Association. They met every other Sunday in Los Angeles, but it wasn't a social club. According to the website, the CSA was primarily set up to help people learn how to sumo.

I had a reporting assignment in Los Angeles the following week, so I told her I'd check it out. Maybe there would be some Japanese contacts there for John. But the truth was that, to me, helping John was secondary. I was intrigued. I had never heard of amateur sumo. I imagined little guys in those padded sumo suits, but the pictures on the website showed men and women wearing spandex under the classic sumo diaper. And they weren't all fat. There were some who looked trim. The website said that the group was created to teach sumo to people of all "sizes, ages, backgrounds, and genders."

Maybe, I thought, *this might be a chance to learn how to be bigger.*

When I showed up at the Jun Chong Martial Arts Center in Santa Monica, a dozen little kids were trying to kill one another while their parents looked on approvingly. At the far end of the room, in a corner, lurked a very large, fat man. Next to him was a jittery guy who was as skinny as me but taller. They looked obviously out of place.

I skirted the kids' tae kwon do class and asked these two if they were with the sumo group. They both smiled. "Fresh meat," said Larry, the big one. The smaller guy stepped forward and introduced himself as Andrew Freund, the founder of the California Sumo Association. His eyes were sunken, his skin sallow, and he wore a motley beard, all of which made him look far older than his thirty-three years. He seemed a little strung out.

In a way, he was. He was addicted to sumo. Andrew had caught the bug while teaching English in Japan in the mid-nineties. He'd go to the beach with Japanese friends, draw a circle in the sand, and wrestle all afternoon. He loved being in the ring so much that he formed the association in 1997 to try to get people to wrestle with him in the United States. Eventually, sumo took over his life. He worked two jobs and poured all his savings into promoting the sport. He slept only four hours a night. "I could have bought a house by now if it weren't for sumo," he said.

After a few faltering years, his efforts started paying off. In 2001, he held the first U.S. Sumo Open on a basketball court at UCLA and drew a crowd of confused students. By 2003, the event had major corporate sponsors, a respectable venue at the Manhattan Beach Country Club, and was featured on ESPN. In January 2004, the *Los*

Angeles Times devoted a Sunday supplement to sumo, detailing a surge in interest and citing hundreds of new competitors.

According to Andrew, amateur sumo was now gaining momentum in the States. Unlike professional sumo, which only exists in Japan, amateur sumo is broken into weight classes, so competitors don't necessarily have to be huge. Of course, the lightweight division is 187 pounds and below, so it doesn't pay to be small. In fact, part of sumo's growing appeal is that it gives overweight people a sport to call their own. As America's population has become increasingly obese, sumo has become more and more appealing. Why slim down to adjust for skinny-people activities when a sport already exists for people of significant girth?

That's why Larry took up the sport. At 285 pounds, he just wasn't enjoying bicycling anymore. He talked about trying other sports, but "that was a hundred pounds ago." Sumo was a sport that welcomed him unconditionally.

"Is sumo time," announced a thirty-year-old Bulgarian named Svetoslav Binev, who had just arrived at the martial arts center. Binev was a two-time amateur sumo world champion who came to California three years ago hoping to do for sumo what Schwarzenegger did for weight lifting. He was the guiding light of the CSA—in addition to being a competitor, he coached the Bulgarian national sumo team and helped spur an eastern European sumo renaissance. It turns out that Bulgaria is a sumo hot spot—bootlegged Japanese sumo tapes have circulated the countryside for the past decade, inspiring a generation of wrestling-centric Slavs like Binev.

Unfortunately, the sumo renaissance wasn't in effect today. No one else showed up—it was just Andrew, Larry, and me. "We have lots of one-on-one instruction today," Binev said as the tae kwon do class let out. He flexed his prodigious muscles. He didn't seem nearly fat enough to be a sumo coach.

"I'm just here to kind of watch and check it out," I said, eyeing Larry's width and Andrew's nervous, twitchy energy. "I'm not sure if I'm sumo material."

"You'll be fine," Andrew said, bouncing up and down on the balls of his feet and leading me onto the mats. He unrolled what looked like a canvas fire hose and started wrapping it around my beach shorts. In a few minutes, I was bare-chested and swaddled in the classic sumo diaper. Binev clapped his hands, raised his leg into the air like a pissing dog, and slammed it down. Larry and Andrew followed suit, so I copied them. We were now all wearing diapers and stomping our feet. This is called *shiko*, Andrew explained. It is a classic sumo exercise that improves balance. Traditionally, it is an intimidating display of weight as large men slam their weight down and shake the ground. But I couldn't manage more than a soft slap when my foot landed. I was a small cymbal crash next to Larry's bass drum rumble.

Andrew went over the basic rules of sumo. You win by either forcing your opponent out of the ring or making him touch the ground inside the ring with anything other than his feet. No eye gouging, groin hits, or hair pulling. And that's it. "So, how 'bout some matches?" he concluded.

"You and Andrew first," Binev said, motioning me into the ring. Andrew talked me through the ritual, which involved some bowing, a few hand gestures to show we had no concealed weapons, and then a staring match in the middle of the ring. Binev said something in Japanese (with a Bulgarian accent) and we went back to the edge of the circle.

"Go for his throat," Binev whispered. "It will throw him off balance."

Andrew slapped his belly lazily, as if it were quite large, though he looked emaciated and jaundiced. Still, I was intimidated. Once again, I had gotten myself in over my head and had no idea what I was doing. But in a moment Binev shouted and Andrew slammed into me. I didn't have time to go for his throat, because he already had his hands on my diaper and was yanking it up. I could feel my balls get cinched, and a wave of anger swept over me. Suddenly, I unleashed a deep faltering yell. It was a strange, foreign voice—one I'd never heard before.

Instinctively, I grabbed Andrew's diaper and yanked him toward the edge. He did the same to me and we began the sumo dance that occurs when opponents spin around and around as they try to hurl each other out of the ring. At the last moment, I pivoted, rolled him over my belly, and smashed him to the ground.

"Wow," Andrew shouted, leaping to his feet. "That was great."

"Very nice," Binev agreed. "You have the fighting spirit."

It's amazing how much fighting spirit wells up when someone starts tugging on your diaper. I felt bigger. I felt completely in control.

"Now we see you and Larry," Binev said.

Larry lumbered over and bowed. I bowed back. Binev signaled the go and I dodged left, pivoted, and drove into Larry as hard as I could. He took two small steps back, recovered, and began a 285-pound steamroll toward me. At the last minute, I squatted low, grabbed his diaper, and rolled him over my right leg. He landed heavily on his back outside the ring and I came spinning down on top of him.

"Fantastic," Binev shouted, slapping me on the back. And though my beginner's luck would soon run out, Andrew told me that if I trained hard, I had a good shot at medaling in my weight class at the U.S. Sumo Open in a few months.

"But first we make you more bigger," Binev said, tapping my bony chest. "You get bruised bone otherwise."

When I got home I had trouble breathing. My arms were streaked with kaleidoscoping yellow and blue bruises and a sneeze hurt so bad I felt like I was going to pass out. My first afternoon of sumo had wreaked havoc on me. We had wrestled for two hours, and both of my opponents had begun beating me consistently by using different techniques. My chest was so bruised I couldn't hug Tara, but I told her proudly that I was going to be a competitor at the U.S. Sumo Open.

She told me that there were certain things that I was just not meant to do. One of them was sumo. "I thought we'd moved beyond doing stupid things," she said.

"I reserved the right to always do stupid things," I said indignantly.

It was the wrong thing to say. Tara had just taken a contracts class at law school and explained to me that agreements needed three things: an offer, acceptance, and consideration. I had made an offer ("I will continue to do stupid things"), but she had not accepted that. Moreover, there was no consideration, which is the legal term for "What's in it for me?" Ergo, no agreement.

"Ergo my ass," I said. "I'm not supporting the two of us so that you can use highfalutin legalese to browbeat me."

Again, the wrong thing to say. Tara pointed out that she had supported me for years while I had engaged in ever more elaborate forms of navel gazing. Now I was trying to say I had greater rights because I was the breadwinner? I was banished to the couch that night to reconsider my point of view.

While I huddled under a thin blanket, I felt the weightiness I had gained in L.A. slipping away. Wrestling had been an intoxicating feeling. It made me feel solid, unshakeable, and sure of myself. I had glimpsed the person I wanted to be: someone secure and grounded. Now I felt small and miserable. I can't focus on anything else when Tara is unhappy. Having kids would make my life that much more complicated—I'd be responsible for their happiness as well. I'd have to be a lot more secure and grounded, which would come as a matter of course as I became a bigger, better sumo wrestler. It upset me that Tara couldn't see how sumo was helping me, but I guess it wasn't immediately obvious to most people.

My mom called the next morning. I had totally forgotten about the sardines. Still, I thought she would appreciate the fact that I was getting deeply involved in sumo. I was bound to make contacts with Japanese people at some point. Also, I could investigate the Soviet-bloc option.

"Has John considered selling his fish in eastern Europe?" I asked, explaining that Binev was a big name in Bulgaria and could maybe be talked into some kind of sponsorship deal.

"What do you mean you have a sumo coach from Bulgaria?" she demanded. "Is this a joke?"

I explained that I was on something akin to a spiritual quest, which she couldn't fault me for. She was constantly going on meditation retreats in northern California to center herself. "Some meditate, others sumo," I said.

"Meditation and sumo are not the same thing, Josh," she replied testily.

"Sumo's a martial art," I replied. "And martial arts are spiritual."

The conversation devolved into an argument over the spirituality of violence. My mom has been meditating since the late seventies, and over the years developed a debilitating response to aggression. She can't watch movies with guns—they make her physically ill. If she sees a photo of a boxer in the morning paper, it upsets her so much, she has trouble getting out of bed. The fact that I was participating in something a few steps removed from boxing horrified her.

To reassure her and buttress my argument that sumo could be spiritual, I cited the wartime setting of the Bhagavad-Gita, the Hindu epic poem that she meditated on daily. She hung up on me.

Despite the disapproval of my family, I pressed ahead and, little by little, a transformation took place in me. On Binev's recommendation, I stopped jogging and began eating as much as I could. At the beginning, I weighed 128. Within a month, I was up to 132.

Of course, I still had a ways to go. The lightweight division was 187 pounds or less, and the closer a competitor was to the cutoff the better. That left me with five weeks to gain another fifty pounds. I began eating two lunches and two dinners every day. It made me very social because I don't like to eat alone. With first and second lunches and dinners to fill up, I caught up with a lot of old friends, and simultaneously began putting on the pounds.

I spent every other weekend in L.A. training with Andrew, Larry, Binev, and a steady stream of novice and experienced wrestlers. I

could feel my moves improving, though the bruises on my chest only worsened. But I was encouraged by a few wins against some of the bigger guys.

In the middle of March, a month before the U.S. Sumo Open, Andrew called me at home. He sounded a little nervous and explained that every year a Japanese sumo star is the guest of honor at the Open. This year Andrew managed to get Musashimaru (a.k.a. Maru, or "Moose"), a Hawaiian who moved to Japan when he was eighteen and was one of only two Yokozuna, or grand champions, in the world. In the two hundred years that records have been kept, Maru holds the title for most consecutive wins and is considered one of the top ten sumo wrestlers of all time. The problem was, Andrew didn't have anyone to drive him during his weeklong visit. The problem ran deeper. Maru was first due to fly to Washington, D.C., as a guest of the Japan-America Society. He was going to be one of the star attractions at this year's National Cherry Blossom Festival, which marked the 150th anniversary of relations between Japan and America. But, again, the society was short-staffed and didn't have anyone to pick Maru up at the airport and take him to all the events.

"So you have a flexible schedule, right?" Andrew asked. "Do you think there's any way you'd be able to drive him around D.C. and L.A. for eight days?"

A 530-pound man has a strange effect on his environment. Before Maru pushed through the arrival doors at Dulles Airport in Washington, D.C., all the light seeping through the edges blacked out. When the doors opened, he completely filled the gap. He was wearing a velour sweat suit made by I.B.M., a Japanese street-wear brand otherwise known as International Black Man. He was followed by a personal hairdresser (obligatory company for a Yokozuna), who carried his tiny Louis Vuitton backpack. A plastic tag on the bag announced in Japanese that it belonged to the "grand champion."

Earlier, while I was waiting for him, I practiced my bowing and

Tyler Tuione

ran over the instructions Andrew had given me: be extremely re-
spectful; bow, but don't overdo the bowing; refer to him as Oyakata,
which means "master"; treat the hairdresser with great respect; the
Oyakata would also be traveling with a manager—refer questions to
him. I spent a number of minutes trying to decide how many bows
would constitute overdoing it. Andrew hadn't specified.

I started bowing as soon as I saw him and probably overdid it.
Maru took no notice and kept walking until I introduced myself as
his driver. He seemed amused. His eyebrows naturally angled up
over his brutish face, making him look as if he were perpetually surprised by how small others were.

"You?" he said and kept walking.

I hurriedly shook hands with Ito-San, the manager, who was in his late thirties and had a cauliflower ear. Ken, the hairdresser, was in his late twenties and had extremely messy hair. Both of them were pudgy and short—they looked like tabletop collectible versions of the big guy when they stood next to him.

Maru took up most of the backseat in the Ford Excursion I had rented. He didn't talk much and looked generally pissed off. He later told me that he had been harassed by the immigration people. It started when they wanted to know his occupation, which he thought was a stupid question. "What does it look like I do?" he said. "You see my hair? You see how big I am? Take a guess." Since Ito-San and Ken didn't speak English, Maru bore the brunt of the questions, something he's not accustomed to doing. He prefers to let others answer for him while he glowers at the questioner.

We sat in an uncomfortable silence at first. I was concentrating on the driving, as I had only been to D.C. twice before, and then only briefly. That translated into a certain amount of panic on my part, as I periodically realized that I had no idea where I was going. I imagined being lost on the streets of the capital with a five-hundred-pound man in my backseat. It sounded like a strange nightmare.

To break the silence and my panic, I lamely tried to play the part of the tour guide. "Here's the Washington Monument and the Lincoln Memorial and some other stuff," I said, sweeping my arm vaguely around as we drove past the Mall.

I glanced in the rearview mirror and saw Maru looking at me skeptically. He asked me how I came to be his driver, and I explained that I was a competitor.

"You sumo?" Maru said, surprised. He said something in Japanese and both Ito-San and Ken looked at me.

"I'm in the lightweight division," I clarified.

Maru giggled. It was a high-pitched, nasal laugh that caught me by surprise. In the rearview mirror, I saw him smiling for the first time. He looked like an oversized eight-year-old.

"Little sumo man," he said, shaking his head and giggling again.

"I'm trying to put on weight," I said, somewhat defensively.

"Oh, yeah?" he asked, suppressing his laugh for two seconds before cracking up again.

From that moment on, Maru treated me differently. The very idea of me, the skinny American sumo wrestler, never failed to bring a smile to his face. He relaxed around me and even gave me a nickname. In his laid-back Hawaiian English, Maru began calling me "Bruddah Josh."

As we drove past the White House, Maru rolled down his window. "Hi, Bush," he sang, waving at the White House. "Hi, Bushy bushy bushy!"

"I saw his daddy vomit," he added with a mischievous smile. He had met three past American presidents and had attended the infamous dinner when Bush senior threw up. "It wasn't pretty."

I didn't fully appreciate the stature of my passenger until a few days later, when our SUV was chased for two blocks at the National Cherry Blossom Festival in downtown D.C. One Japanese guy kept trying to push his face through the window, and a number of women hoisted their babies in the air, hoping that Maru would roll down the window and touch the children for good luck. The Japanese regarded him as a near deity, but in public he was taciturn, rarely spoke, and never smiled. He was known for his fierceness in the ring and his reserve outside and seemed to be all the more revered for it.

I was meeting him at a difficult time in his life. When a wrestler achieves the rank of grand champion, he is not allowed to post a losing record. If he does, he is expected to retire. Maru had broken his wrist, started losing, and, in keeping with the tradition, announced that he was officially retiring this coming October. He had had one of the fastest rises through the ranks in sumo history and was only thirty-two, but he already reminisced like an old man.

"I've had a really strange life, bro," he told me the morning after he arrived. It seemed like he wanted to talk to someone, but Ito-San and Ken both worked for him. And in Japan, he's treated like a god so he couldn't really have normal conversations there. Our time in the car was a rare opportunity to hang out and relax, particularly on that first full day. There were no scheduled events—the organizers wanted the Oyakata to have a day to get over his jet lag. But, instead of resting, he wanted to track down a long-lost aunt. She had left Hawaii in the seventies and he had only seen her once in the last twenty years. Now her husband was a colonel at an army base in southern Virginia and she had invited us to come for a visit. It was a three-hour drive each way.

"I was so worried when I first got to Japan," he said as we drove south along the tree-lined interstate. He told me that in high school on Oahu, he had wanted to wrestle on the school's Greco-Roman team. He thought he'd be good at it, but he was disqualified from the first competition for being twenty pounds over the maximum weight. He quit the team and started hanging out with a rough crowd. Soon he was suspended for playing craps in the school yard. His new friends got into fights, but he hung back. "I didn't like the fighting," he said. Even now, he said, he gets nauseous before every competition.

Football helped him get his young life back in order. He was good at it and was recruited by colleges on the mainland. But his coach introduced him to a sumo recruiter who offered him a three-month trial in Japan. Maru wanted to help support his family, so he accepted, though he knew almost nothing about the sport. They were offering him a career, not just four years in college. But his main concern at the time was more prosaic: "I just didn't want to show everybody my butt."

Maru constantly surprised me. About twenty minutes into the drive, he shyly asked me what kind of music I liked. When I said I was open to anything, he pulled out a CD from his Louis Vuitton backpack. It was a mix of Abba tunes, the *Grease* soundtrack, and Rupert Holmes's piña colada song.

When the exuberant piano glissando announced Abba's "Dancing Queen," the Oyakata started humming along in his squeaky, nasal tone. The hairdresser began tapping his foot in the passenger seat next to me. I couldn't help but smile, and when the chorus hit, we were all singing "You are the dancing queen!"

Egg rolls, chicken wings, coleslaw, two whole fish, steak, corn, boiled shrimp, a vanilla sponge cake, and a two-foot-tall bowl of layered triple-chocolate cake (brownies, pound cake, and pudding with Cool Whip separating the layers). Almost immediately upon our arrival at Maru's aunt's house, she laid out a massive Samoan-themed feast, and Maru insisted I sit at the head of the table.

"Bruddah Josh is a sumo wrestler," Maru said, introducing me to his aunt as he gave her a hug. "He just don't look it yet."

She was about five feet four inches and no more than 120 pounds and seemed to disappear inside Maru's prodigious embrace. He called her "Auntie" and hugged her so tight, I was afraid he'd hurt her. She smiled at me from a gap in his fat and, almost in tears, thanked me for reuniting her with her nephew.

Ito-San patted me on the back. "Tanka you," he said, surprising me with his hidden English. "Very nice you to be with us."

I tried to get him to sit at the head of the table. I was just the driver, after all, but Ito-San took his cues from the way Maru acted with me. He seemed to think that having me around was good for Maru and treated me almost as deferentially as he treated the big man. It was embarrassing. He was twenty years older and deserved far more respect than I did. I tried bowing and gesturing at the table. He bowed back. We ended up in a bow-a-thon, and since we were drawing attention to ourselves, I finally sat down.

From the outside, it would have been impossible to tell that anything unusual was happening within the staid white Colonial-style house on the edge of the base. But inside, the American military and northern Virginia were left behind. We were now in the Pacific islands. All the blinds were drawn. The walls provided the view: vibrant floor-to-ceiling color photos of Hawaiian and Samoan beaches covered almost every bare space. The gaps were filled with Samoan war clubs, tropical wooden instruments, and a small shrine to Maru by the door. The air smelled of frying fish and tuberose.

"We try to make it like the islands," Auntie told Maru as he inhaled handful after handful of baby chicken wings. "But you're lucky. You can move back to Hawaii now that you're retiring."

Maru wasn't sure that he would. He thought his mom would feed him too much and he desperately wanted to lose weight.

"When I came to Japan, I weighed 280," he said. "I put on almost twenty pounds a year for fifteen years. I don't think it's going to be as easy to lose. But we need to fatten Bruddah Josh up. Maybe I just give him some of my belly." He laughed loudly. "Either that or we barbecue him for lunch," he said, explaining that his Samoan ancestors had once been cannibals.

"You better keep your eyes on Auntie," he warned. "She might look small, but if she needs an extra appetizer, she might put you in the salad."

I considered this. "Who's going to drive you back to D.C. if you eat me?" I asked.

"Good point. Auntie, don't barbecue Bruddah Josh."

As it turned out, there was no shortage of food. After my second helping of triple-chocolate cake, I tried to deflect Ito and the cake spoon. He had been dishing me food incessantly.

"No more cake," I said, as clearly as I could. Maru said something in Japanese and Ito made a quick move with the spoon. Another heap of cake jiggled on my plate.

"Ito was a karate champ," Maru said. "He's fast. Eat up."

"I'm so impressed that somebody your size is competing," Auntie said encouragingly. "That's very brave. Have you ever won a match?"

I explained that I had a shot against the guys in the lightweight division, but I almost always lost to the big guys. Maru pushed himself up.

"We're going to fix that right now," he said, shouting an order at Ken, who leaped to his feet. Maru explained that there was a very good technique a small guy could use to beat someone much larger. Following Maru's instructions, Ken grabbed the back of Maru's prodigious shorts, wedged himself under his boss's hanging stomach, and used a hip as a pivot point to roll the Oyakata in a semicircle. Once he got Maru moving, Ken took a stutter step forward, extended his leg, and Maru tripped over it, almost smashing into the dining room table. It was a revelation. I imagined myself wrestling Larry and could see how I'd lay him out.

"You get it?" Maru asked, recovering his composure.

"Yeah, it's great."

"Good. Now go take a nap," Maru said, explaining that sleeping immediately after eating is the best way to turn food into fat.

I dutifully followed his aunt upstairs. She pointed out the bathroom, which had a scale in it. I stepped on and registered 143 pounds. I was up 11 pounds for the week. I reckoned I had put on at least 5 of those pounds in the last three hours of eating.

Auntie pointed me to a bedroom accented with pictures of vivid blue waves and white-sand beaches. My belly ached but I was glad that Maru accepted me as a wrestler. I fell asleep immediately and dreamed of giant, cresting waves of Cool Whip.

Andrew arrived the following day with three top amateur American sumo stars. They were scheduled to perform sumo demonstrations throughout the weekend for the Cherry Blossom Festival and all of them were gold-medal favorites for next week's U.S. Sumo Open. Troy Collins, the lightest, was a six-foot-two-inch, 245-pound Los Angeles cop who wrote his sumo training off as a job expense

("If I need to drop somebody on the job, you'll see some sumo in action"). Collins was joined by fellow middleweight Kena Heffernan, a twenty-nine-year-old Hawaiian who had been a standout tailback on the Yale football team. Tyler Tuione, a.k.a. "Big T," rounded out the triumvirate at six feet four inches and 520 pounds.

The first stop was Independence Plaza, a civic space a few hundred yards from the White House. Andrew was wearing a wrinkled suit and periodically pretended to slam-dunk an imaginary basketball into an imaginary hoop. Maru was expected to make a speech before each demonstration so I dropped him off at the plaza, parked the car, and ran back.

"Hey, you better get changed," Andrew told me when I trotted up to the plaza. Throngs of people were already crowded around a raised stage where Japanese sword-fighting experts demonstrated their talents. "You're on in ten minutes."

Before I'd left for D.C., Andrew had told me that I'd learn a lot from watching the demonstrations. He hadn't told me I'd be in them. Ten minutes later I was standing beside the stage, barefoot and half-naked in a sumo diaper. The audience of six hundred was bundled up against the 40-degree weather. The bigger guys had layers of protective fat—I started shivering immediately. From where I was standing, I could see a section of the White House and wondered if the president was watching.

We started out with a few *shiko*, the side-to-side sumo stomp. I watched Kena and tried to learn from his movements. I could feel the familiar tunneling return. I forgot about the cold and the crowd and the president. We were entering sumo land.

"Let's play catch now," Kena said quietly so the audience couldn't hear. Kena pointed at me. "Charge me as hard as you can and I'll catch you."

We started at the edge of the ring and I slammed into him. He resisted lightly so that I could push him across the ring. It was a classic sumo exercise. In Japan, younger wrestlers are expected to shove their elders around the ring like this until they throw up. It builds endurance while allowing the more seasoned wrestlers to coach by feel.

It wasn't hard to push Kena, but trying to attack Big T was another thing entirely. Crouching down in front of him was like standing at the base of a very large breaking wave. Still, I hit him hard at the go and advanced my feet like Kena said. Big T shuddered—his fat rippled backward, ricocheted off the far side of his body, and came rushing back toward me. The crowd went crazy as his breasts whiplashed into my face, slapping my head to the left. After three steps, I was sunk in man fat, but Big T kept backing up. He let me win, sending the crowd into an ecstasy of cheering.

The following day, we did more sumo demonstrations at the Washington Hilton. We were put in a subterranean conference room at the end of a very long hall. It was hard to find, so there were never more than a dozen people there at any given time. Maru felt more comfortable and informed me that it was time to work on my *tachiai,* my sumo charge. Ken helped him into a pair of shorts, and Maru crouched slightly, his hands on his thighs. Then he instructed me to hit him as if it were the U.S. Sumo Open. The spectators—a bunch of high school students studying Japanese—were expecting a lecture on the history of sumo. What they got was me smashing into Maru and recoiling. It felt like colliding with a bag of cement.

While I wrestled Maru, Kena narrated, describing me as "rock solid." But Maru undermined that analysis when he told me that I was "leaping like a skinny man." He instructed me to squat lower, advance my feet, and use my weight. "None of this leaping stuff."

To demonstrate, he said he would charge me. I took a deep breath. Not many people get to experience the charge of a grand champion. I readied myself, and he slammed into me with his head down. The air left my lungs with a whoosh, and for an instant I was airborne. But I was gaining weight, both physically and mentally, and I landed on the ground with an impressive thud.

"It's all about learning how to use your weight," Maru said.

The Japanese ambassador was a dapper, gray-haired man with oversized glasses. He didn't really want to talk to me, particularly about sardines, but I had come to his house with Musashimaru, one of his country's greatest sumo wrestlers, so he had to listen.

"When the sardines leave Japan, you're going to be in a fix," I explained to him. "People are going to want the fish, and, as a politician, if you can't give it to them, that's a problem."

"Uh," the ambassador said, looking around nervously for an aide.

"But I've got a solution for you: Oregon sardines. Nice, fresh Pacific sardines, canned and shipped to Tokyo. What do you think?"

"It's a very interesting idea," he allowed. "But I really am late for another meeting."

I told him that I'd have my stepdad follow up with him. We shook hands and someone took our picture. The photograph shows me smiling confidently while the ambassador appears bewildered. I had waylaid him at a private Cherry Blossom Festival reception he was holding at his home. It was awkward to bring up the sardine issue but it was also my big opportunity to help John out. I laid the groundwork as best I could. The ambassador's people could open a lot of doors.

I called John that night to tell him the good news, but he was in the throes of depression. The latest Oregon fishing reports had just come in. No one was catching any sardines. The exodus had not occurred. Yet again, another of his business plans was in shambles.

Samoan Godfather, the massively tattooed front man for the platinum-selling rap group the Boo Yaa TRIBE, exhaled a web of smoke and squinted at me. He was a former south Los Angeles gang leader, an ex-con, and the man behind such rap songs as "Bury U, Bury Me" and "Pimpin', Playin', Hustlin'." I was sitting across a conference table from him at his warehouse in Torrance, California. Two large assistants/bodyguards stood beside him.

Godfather frowned, fingered his ponytails, and ashed his cigarette. He didn't seem like someone who enjoyed meeting new people. He glanced at Maru, who was sitting beside me. Maru had met the Godfather years ago when the TRIBE was touring Japan. He was one of Maru's oldest friends.

"This is my friend Josh," Maru explained. "He's traveling with me."

Godfather seemed to relax a little and asked how Maru was doing. Maru said that his career was coming to an end and that he needed to figure out what to do next. Some retired champions became actors or even singers. Godfather's cousin—a Samoan wrestler named Konishiki—was now the David Hasselhoff of Japan. He was known primarily for wrestling, but a fierce minority felt that his true talent was singing love songs. Godfather suggested that Maru and Konishiki do a duet—he could help them produce it.

But Maru was too shy for that. He didn't even like being in public, let alone performing. He shook his big head. He really didn't know what he was going to do. In the short term, he would help train younger athletes. "Like Josh," he said.

Godfather looked at me and smiled for the first time. "You're going to go far with a teacher like Sale," he said, using Maru's Samoan name. "Trust the Godfather."

The U.S. Sumo Open was held at a hotel in downtown Los Angeles on the first Tuesday of Passover. Andrew said he could only afford to rent the space midweek, but that didn't dissuade people from attending. By seven P.M. the chandeliered ballroom had reached its maximum occupancy of 735 people. Hundreds more were queued up in the hotel lobby, hoping to get in.

Tara flew down from San Francisco to cheer for me and, together with a group of our Los Angeles friends, held up a handmade sign that said GO JOSH! I felt great. There were twenty-three competitors here, seven of them in the lightweight division, and I felt on par with

all of them. It didn't matter to me that the program for the event detailed an intimidating list of accomplishments beside each man's
picture. Most of the lightweights were near the 187-pound limit, and
almost all of them had won medals at previous competitions. The
list of accomplishments beside my picture was blank. I was also the
only one in the photos wearing glasses. But the picture had been
taken a month ago, and I was bigger now. It was hard to get ahead of
my metabolism, but in the long run I had managed to gain 6
pounds—I was up to 134. Most important, I *felt* substantially larger.

As I waited in the area roped off for competitors, I felt a flash of
discomfort. For the first time, I was wearing the *mawashi* with
nothing underneath and everyone could see my ass. I had night-
mares about the thing falling off, so I tied it too tight and now it was
crushing my nuts and making me nauseous. I tried to nonchalantly
pull it down a bit, but I couldn't bring myself to fidget with my
crotch in front of so many people.

Maru arrived to a great cheer, said hello into the microphone, and
Andrew announced the beginning of the 2004 U.S. Sumo Open. I
was scheduled to compete in both the lightweight and openweight
divisions to maximize my chances of winning, but my lightweight
matches went by in a blur of limbs and heavy impacts. I was too excited, too keyed up, and kept leaping off the start and extending my
center of gravity. The one thing I hadn't learned was how to stay
calm during a major sumo tournament.

My opponents—a Mongolian, a lawyer, a UCLA student—sensed
that I wasn't grounded. They came at me low and repeatedly drove
me backward and out of the ring. But with each match I gained a
measure of confidence, and by the time I was called up for the openweight division I was calm.

"Stop leaping," Maru quietly demanded as I waited by the referees' table. "Do how I taught you now."

Andrew announced the first pairing. On the left side, Marcus Barber was called up. Barber, a 460-pound opera singer, looked like an

avalanche waiting to happen. The crowd started clapping in unison—the openweight division was the main event—but they suddenly fell silent when I stepped forward.

"And on the other side of the ring," Andrew purred through the mike, "at 134 pounds, we have the lightest man to ever sumo at the U.S. Open."

I popped in my mouth guard and trotted out to the ring. The paramedics in the corner stood up. I could hear murmurs of concern, but almost immediately the atmosphere started to change. Though Barber weighed more than three times what I did, the audience sensed something. They could feel that there was some other force at play here. And they were right. I might have looked skinny, but somehow the aura of a fat man emanated from me. I slapped my wiry stomach. The crowd started chanting my name.

If Barber was intimidated, he didn't show it. He was one of North America's best heavyweight sumo wrestlers and was known for his stability. He was almost impossible to knock over. We bowed, squatted in the middle of the ring, and stared into each other's faces. We were only a few feet apart.

To show I wasn't scared, I looked right through him, as though I could see that he was really a little man on the inside. I thought I saw him wobble slightly as the referee stepped into the ring and told us to prepare to attack. I backed up a few steps, squatted at the start line, and ground my left fist into the ground. Then, slowly, I lowered my right fist to the mat. Barber was all mine.

"*Hakkeyoi!*" the ref shouted to start the match, and I dodged low, avoiding Barber's massive flailing arms. He stepped toward me, but I slipped past him, latching on to the back of his diaper like Maru had taught me. I had made it.

Barber was momentarily stunned that I had the advantage. The audience went crazy. I shoved myself under his stomach, stuck my leg out, and pulled as hard as I could on Barber's backside.

In theory, this was when he was supposed to stumble forward and trip over my outstretched leg. I would then humbly bow and accept victory. But he didn't budge. I pulled again and felt a rising panic. The clarity I had felt over the past few minutes began to blur. I couldn't move Barber. As his arms strained to reach my diaper, I tried pulling myself into a defensive position behind him. It didn't work. He latched on to the diaper, heaved me into the air, and carried me out of the ring on his stomach.

I was defeated. I had lost every single match and now my testicles ached intensely. As Barber deposited me gently on the ground, it all seemed suddenly meaningless. I went 0 for 7. Who was I fooling? I was a skinny loser. As I slinked off to a corner, I was so depressed I could barely stand up.

Like my grandpa and mom before me, I couldn't deliver. I had plenty of questions but no answers. So what would I tell my kids? How could I answer their questions about life? I knew nothing and I didn't subscribe to any religion, so I didn't have any ready-made responses.

An eight-year-old boy and his father approached me in the corner. I frowned but the boy timidly held out his program and asked if I would sign it. I thought it was a joke, but the kid kept holding out the program, so I sullenly took it and asked why he wanted my autograph. After all, I had just lost everything.

The kid looked nervously at his shoes. He was too shy to say.

"Because you had the most fighting spirit," his father said quickly to end his son's embarrassment. "You should have given up but you didn't and that meant a lot to my son."

In the next ten minutes, a half dozen people asked for my autograph, and it slowly dawned on me that maybe this wasn't a complete defeat. I had unwittingly inspired these people and that made me feel better. Being in the ring hurt—I would be bruised for two weeks—but the image of me fighting Barber would be with that little boy for a long time. Maybe it would help him.

I was still depressed but I had to admit that I had come a long way from when I weighed 128 pounds. I might not have been fluent in the language of weight yet, but I could definitely hold a conversation and that had given me the ability to ask a new, critical question: What would happen when I stopped being the questioner and became the questioned? What sorts of answers did I have?

Maru looked up from his own, much larger mob of autograph seekers and waved me over. "Bruddah Josh," he said, "you fought hard. We just gotta get you a little fatter."

Stefano Morselli

CHAPTER FOUR

THE GOLDEN
SHRIMP

To gain weight for the U.S. Sumo Open, I had been eating five to six meals a day and had stopped jogging. I was consuming nearly four thousand calories a day, not exercising, and I still only gained six pounds over four months. I have a fast metabolism but not that fast. My theory was that my latent angst had been consuming at least one thousand calories a day, storing up energy to wage a full-on assault.

After the tournament, it attacked. Getting out of bed became a battle. I felt drained, depressed, and I had no direction. At a time when I needed answers, I was overwhelmed by questions. Was I losing my curiosity because I made a living off it? Was I balding? Would I ever be able to afford an apartment with light, a dining room, and a bathtub? Did I need a haircut?

I cut back on the food to try to flush the angst. I had been so happy with the direction of my life before. Now I felt a pervasive malaise. I started running again. I wanted to pound myself into submission, to weaken the depression so I could get the upper hand, but all that pounding hurt my knees. My body was not used to jogging with those extra few pounds. I was forced to limit my running and the angst lingered.

I searched online for ways to help reduce knee pain while jogging and came across a curious website. "Welcome to the Universe of Retro Movements," it proclaimed. It was devoted to the concept that moving backward was not only better for your joints but better for the world. According to Christian Grollé, the site's French creator, the modern world had willfully suppressed our need to move backward. Grollé believed that this was a leading cause of depression and laziness. "If you are tired of life, emotionally depressed, or depleted of energy, alternate," he wrote. "That is to say, for a moment, do the opposite of what you were doing. You will see the results for yourself."

It was like he was speaking directly to me. I was depressed, and whatever I was doing now, it wasn't working. I anxiously kept reading, waiting for more insight. The home page featured a photo of a man named Dick Fosbury doing the high jump at the 1968 Olympics in Mexico City. The caption read, "Backward jumping: A great revolution in athletics." Beneath the photo, a paragraph explained that before Dick Fosbury, everyone tried to straddle the high-jump bar like they do in a steeplechase. Then this Oregonian named Fosbury came along and said he'd break all the records by jumping backward. People called it the Fosbury Flop and thought he was crazy. "If kids try to imitate Fosbury," groused the U.S. Olympic coach, "he'll wipe out an entire generation of high jumpers because they'll all have broken necks."

But then Fosbury made the Olympic team with his wild style and went on to shatter both the American and the Olympic high-jump records. Now everybody jumps the high bar backward.

For Grollé, backward running was the beachhead for the retro movement, which he referred to as a "great revolution." Everybody could run backward. It was easy to understand, fun to do, and better for your health. To support his claim, he referenced biomechanical studies compiled by professors at the University of Oregon, the birthplace of Nike. The studies indicated a long list of backward-running benefits. Reduced knee strain was high on the list.

But this was not just about knee pain. That was just the tip of the iceberg. In fact, according to Grollé, backward running was the fastest way to approach the true but hidden meaning of life.

"The emergence of backward running is not a matter of chance," Grollé wrote. "It is both a sign and the symbol that something 'in the air' is becoming reversed. This new way of running announces the beginning of a new civilization."

This guy had really been getting a lot out of his running. Or maybe he just dropped too much acid in college. But in my gut, I felt that he was on to something.

"What could be more effective than this simple exercise to modify our view of everything? It can change our human relationships, our relationship to money, our conception of time, and at the social level can alter the face of our cities, our transportation and exchange systems."

Exchange systems? I spent five minutes pondering the relationship between backward running and international trade. It was not a productive use of my time, but I was fascinated. Maybe I just didn't understand it because I hadn't tried it.

I immediately laced up my shoes and ran forward to Aquatic Park, a long, pedestrians-only pathway along the waterfront in San Francisco. The path curves out onto a paved pier favored by Chinese fishermen and joggers. I had run it countless times, but it never occurred to me to run it backward.

I flipped around and started trotting backward. To do it, I had to elevate myself on the balls of my feet and basically dance backward across the ground. Since I was up on my tiptoes, my calves bore the brunt of the workout, acting like a dampening coil and taking most of the shock off my knees. Plus, my heels weren't thudding into the ground. It was a much more elegant and graceful movement, and, though it was exhausting, it didn't hurt my knees. The downside was that I couldn't run more than a half mile before my calves gave out.

Still, I found it exhilarating, because the fundamental problem with running backward is that you can't see where you're going. Potholes, fishhooks, other joggers, Porta Potties, tourists, and fish carcasses—in that order—were the obstacles I contended with. It was worth it. I felt like I was entering uncharted territory where the challenges were all new. People have been running forward for thousands of years. The original marathon runner, Philippides, did his thing twenty-five hundred years ago. We were long past due for a change. As far as I knew, backward running had no benchmarks; it had yet to establish its own marathon. In a world where almost everything had been done before, backward running was so new it was sparkling.

I became a convert. Backward running would be my new religion; it gave me a visceral way to struggle with uncertainty. I was constantly afraid of what was ahead of me while running backward because I couldn't see it, but that was precisely the fear I was contending with in my day-to-day life. I had too many questions without answers. Backward running let me attack the uncertainty and fear in a concrete way.

But it was difficult to fight the battle alone. I was often scared running in reverse along the water, weaving and dodging backward between the fishing lines. I realized that it would be a lot easier if I had someone to commiserate with, but I suspected that none of my friends would understand the allure of running backward. I was forced to use the persona of a forward runner to attract them. I'd nonchalantly mention to old friends that I was running again and arrange to go jogging some morning. We'd hit the pavement and after a mile or two I'd say something about backward running. Most looked at me like I was crazy.

"Come on, just try it," I'd say.

Usually they would try it but would burst out laughing after a few yards and turn forward again. They'd think I was joking and I'd have to hide my disappointment and laugh with them. I wouldn't run with them again. I'd say my knees still hurt.

To sustain myself, I returned frequently to Grollé's website. It was surprisingly well developed. He had already made ten proposals to the International Olympic Committee regarding an Olympic backward-running event and there was even a section devoted to "Tandem Running." The image showed a man and a woman running face-to-face—one forward, the other backward. "A New Way of Running for Couples," it said. I clicked on the link and was taken to a page of videos that showed attractive men and women moving languidly, their gaits identical and their eyes locked. It was quite sexy.

When Tara came home from school, I suggested we give it a try. She never enjoyed running with me because I go too fast for her. The beauty of tandem running was that I ran much slower when I was going backward. After I showed her the hypnotic sexual jogging imagery on the website, she agreed.

We ran the five blocks down to the water and then I started "retrorunning"—the term Grollé had assigned to the new sport. It was a sunny day and a light breeze brought the smell of salt water off the bay. It felt good. Tara and I were staring into each other's eyes like we were making love. I had to trust that she would guide me as I moved backward. Our bodies synchronized. Our hips moved together, as if we were salsa dancing at high speed. I started to get a hard-on. The tourists stopped strolling to ogle us and the sunbathers on the narrow beach turned to watch. It was like we had invited Fisherman's Wharf into our bedroom. I got embarrassed.

"Why'd you stop?" Tara complained when I turned around, transforming us instantly back into normal people.

"It was a little obscene," I said.

"What was?"

"That."

"What?"

"The two of us, just now."

"What are you talking about?"

"Didn't you feel anything?"

"I felt something in my calf."

Okay, so it hadn't been a sexual experience for her. She enjoyed it, but mainly because we were able to run together. We tried it again and this time I studiously avoided looking into her eyes. Now I fixated on her bouncing tits and once again had to stop. When you run forward with someone, you're usually shoulder-to-shoulder, staring out at the scenery ahead. But tandem running gives you nothing to look at besides your partner's heaving, sweaty body.

When we got home, Tara fended off my kisses and groping hands. She wanted to call her aunt in India before the workday began over there. I tried undressing her while the phone rang, but when Poornima picked up Tara kicked me in the shin and I retreated to the kitchen to find some ice. I figured I might make her feel bad with the ice and win some sympathy sex.

"Everything's fine here," Tara said to her aunt and glared at me. "Josh has gotten really into backward running."

She was quiet for a second, nodded her head, and said, "Oh, really?" Then she handed me the phone.

Poornima is a ball-busting woman wrapped tightly in a silk sari. She has a Ph.D. in marketing and teaches at a university in southern India. She is Tara's youngest aunt and is a woman who knows what's best for you, whether or not you agree. "Do you expect to be making any money in the near future?" she liked to ask me.

I was expecting some iteration of this when I picked up the phone. Even though I was supporting Tara now, we weren't exactly doing great. Poornima was concerned that I wasn't providing well enough for her niece, and she often let me know it.

But today, to my surprise, she asked if I knew about the backward runner in Chennai. I didn't. According to Poornima, the local newspaper had run an article about a man who broke the Guinness World Record for distance covered in twenty-four hours of continuous backward running. Better yet, he worked as a dish-towel salesman down the street from Poornima's house. I asked her to get his phone number for me and passed the phone back to Tara.

I checked online and, sure enough, on a site called Chennaibest

.com, an article chronicled the accomplishments of world-class backward runner K. Veerabadran from Chennai, India. It first detailed how he logged 85 backward miles in twenty-four hours and then pointed out that he also set a forward-walking record by covering 380 miles in five continuous days. He didn't even sleep. At the end of the five days he was a walking zombie and kept himself going by gnawing raw chilies until his mouth blistered. In the photo accompanying the article, he was a short balding man standing unhappily in an alley with a ballpoint pen in his shirt pocket. It seemed like he was just sent out to empty the office garbage. He looked like a career clerk who was always getting shit on by management. The article also mentioned that Veerabadran didn't start running, forward or backward, until he was forty, which made me think that he had a midlife crisis after being asked to make tea one too many times. But his running career appeared to have ended. While gunning for a new backward record, he was run over by a truck that he probably never saw coming. Amazingly, he wasn't seriously injured, but he declared that he wouldn't try to break his own record again until someone else did.

I showed the article to Tara and she focused on the part about Veerabadran getting run over. She said that running backward was dangerous and insisted that I wear a helmet.

"There's no way," I said. "I'm not going to let you make me look like a fool."

"You already look like a fool running backward," she retorted. "The helmet's not going to change anything."

The next morning, we went to a bike shop on the edge of the Haight-Ashbury district. "He needs a helmet," Tara told the saleswoman. She was young, blond, pierced, and tattooed and wore thick black eyeliner.

"What kind of biking do you do?" she asked me.

I explained that I was a backward runner and my wife thought I was going to trip and smash my head or get run over by a truck like this famous backward runner in India.

"Did you say *backwood* or *backward*?" the saleswoman asked.

"I said *backward*."

"Okay, good," she said. She didn't look like the type of girl who was surprised by much. "Well, let me show you what we have."

In a minute, the saleswoman and I were lying flat on our backs banging our heads on the cement floor. The helmets had a problem: they didn't cover the back of the head.

"That's a problem if you fall backward," she said, looking across the floor at me. "And if you get hit by a truck, this ain't gonna help you."

When we got home empty-handed, I fired up the backward-running website to show Tara that no one else wore a helmet. I clicked on a link I had previously overlooked titled "Retrorunning Races Around the World." There was a picture of five Taoist monks in China's Wudang Mountains jogging backward. They all wore Nefertiti-style hats.

"See!" Tara shouted. "The monks know what's good for them."

"They're just caps. They wouldn't help in a fall."

"How do you know?"

"Look at them!" I shouted back. "They don't even cover the back of the head."

I quickly scrolled down to prevent any further commentary on the monks and was rewarded with a list of international backward-running races. Pictures showed dozens of people participating, none of whom wore a helmet. Tara walked away in frustration while I became engrossed in this new treasure trove of information.

The oldest continuously held race was the "Gambero d'Oro"— the Golden Shrimp. Founded in 1992 in Italy, it looked very serious. The thirty-five runners pictured were fitted in racing tank tops and there were at least four teams in matching track suits. They all looked trim and happy. In the background, the Italian countryside glowed golden and blue. There was an e-mail contact, so I tapped a quick note asking for more information. These were the types of people I had been looking for.

The next morning, there was an e-mail in my in-box from someone named Paolo Pessina. "Hullo, Joshua," he wrote. "I am Paolo Pessina, organizer of the Golden Shrimp backward race in Poviglio, the first in Europe. This year it will be a very big village feast. We should be very happy for you to present yourself to our race. We help you in everything you need. Do you like backward running? Write me. I answer you with pleasure."

"Dear Paolo," I immediately wrote back. "I love to run backward but haven't found anyone else who likes it. Do you know of any backward runners in America? Are there many backward runners in Italy? How many come to your race? Tell me more about it. I would like to meet other people who run backward."

Paolo responded that retrorunning was one of the hottest new sports in Italy. There was a race almost every weekend from April to October, though his attracted the most runners and was considered the de facto backward-running world championship. For his race this July, he expected 150 retrorunners from all over Europe. The course was three kilometers and the record was held by an Italian named Stefano Morselli, who covered the distance in 12:48 minutes. That translates into an astounding 6:45-minutes-per-mile pace. Running forward that fast is hard.

There were clearly people who were leading the charge into this new world and I wanted to be one of them. Not only because it was exciting but because Grollé's words spoke to me. I believed him when he said that retrorunning could lead me to a new way of existing in the world. It was exactly what I was looking for.

But it wasn't my style to continue running on my own here in San Francisco. If I was going to push boundaries, I wanted to push them as far as I could, and that meant competing against the best retrorunners in the world. That, in turn, meant flying to Italy to retrorun the Golden Shrimp. I realized, though, that if I wanted to learn the secrets of retrorunning, I had to be worthy of them. I had to become not just a good retrorunner but one of the best.

I didn't tell Tara about my e-mail exchange with Pessina. Before I started flying around the world, I needed to see if I was competitive.

This would arm me with the ammunition I would need to defend what she would surely view as a rash and expensive decision.

I jumped on the scooter that afternoon and drove over to Kezar Stadium, San Francisco's historic public track. It's historic mainly because it's featured prominently in *Dirty Harry*, in which Clint Eastwood muttered, "You've got to ask yourself one question: 'Do I feel lucky?' Well, do ya, punk?"

Actually, I *was* feeling lucky as I stretched out. There were some serious-looking runners hurtling around the oval, but their calves didn't look as good as mine. Months of backward running had made my calves bulge out. These hotshots might do okay putting one foot in front of the other, but they would collapse as soon as they tried putting one behind the other.

I felt good at the beginning. I took the inside lane and was moving fast, but I didn't really have a good sense of distance. Three kilometers was a little more than seven laps—I hadn't run that far backward all at once. It was also strange to be running on a track with so many people. When you're running backward, you watch people gain on you. It's an aggressive form of tandem running because they're staring ahead and you're staring back. On the straightaways, it's like watching someone come to kick your ass.

It made me run even faster, which wasn't a good thing. After two laps, I hit the proverbial wall. It's the point where you lose your runner's high and segue into runner's hell. The pain in my legs and lungs turned from a mild burn to a thousand-acre wildfire. My body began screaming for me to stop running. When I ran a marathon eight years ago, I hit the wall after two hours. Backward running got me there in five minutes.

For me, the wall is a fascinating (though obviously unpleasant) place to be. It's a mental space where the body and the mind do battle. I treat it as a test: Can my mind order my body to keep moving? Slowing down would definitely decrease the pain, but as I chugged backward I knew that I wouldn't stand up to Morselli's record if I began to lag. The whole point was to ignore the throb in my legs.

I was in I'm-going-to-die-soon pain by lap four. My calves felt like they were burning through my skin and my feet were aching from the high-speed pounding. I was having trouble staying up on my tip-toes. I started to lower my heels a bit but they caught on the ground and made me stumble. The stumbling was terrible because it took extra energy to keep myself from crashing to the ground. Each stumble depleted me more and I couldn't help but slow down. My knees were fine, but the rest of me was falling apart.

By the time I came to the end of the seventh and final lap, I looked like a ninety-year-old man backing up to the toilet for his morning shit. I was moving, but just barely. When I crossed the finish line, I tried to turn around but there was no strength left in my hip flexors. My body buckled and I hit the ground. The hotshot runners darted around me as I shamelessly crawled to the edge of the track. I looked at my watch, which I had stopped when I crossed the line. My time was 22:17 minutes. I was ten minutes off the record.

I wasn't in the same league as Morselli. I wasn't even in the same universe. I felt almost as ridiculous as the guy dancing around the outside edge of the track in a faded red bikini. At least he had headphones on and was in his own world. I was painfully aware of how fast everyone else was running. The forward runners were probably moving at Morselli's pace, a speed that appeared unattainable for me.

But then I started to rationalize my performance. *It's only my first timed run*, I said to myself. *And if a human can run that fast, and I am a human, then I can do it.* The logic started to convince me. *Why can't I do it? Should I just accept that my legs or heart isn't good enough? Who says I have to accept my limitations? In fact, fuck it. I don't accept them.*

I felt better. I had a new mission and missions always excite me. If I had done better, I don't think I would have been as energized as I was now. The fact that I had done so poorly was like an insult, like everyone was laughing at me because I was so pathetic. "Oh, yeah?" I wanted to say. "I'll show you." It was the classic response of a kid who feels picked on. My shitty performance guaranteed that I was going to stick with it, just to prove them all wrong. My depression had lifted.

Tara handed me a scrap of paper when I got home. "Poornima called with this," she said. "It's the backward guy. She stopped by his shop and got his number."

I checked the time. It was morning in India so I dialed the number. The long, static-filled rings of India buzzed through the handset a few times and then someone picked up the line and shouted unintelligibly. I asked for Mr. Veerabadran.

"Yes, yes, yes," the voice screamed. I had to hold the handset away from my ear. "This is Veerabadran."

"My name is Joshua Davis," I said. "I'm a backward runner."

I sounded like an alcoholic looking for a sponsor. "I heard about your backward running," I said awkwardly.

"I am Veerabadran!" the guy screamed again.

"The backward runner?"

"I am sixty years old."

"Okay," I said, and paused, expecting him to say something else. Finally, I added: "I'd love to know more about your backward running."

"I have willpower," he shouted. "I have only willpower."

"Do you still run backward?"

"Four hundred kilometers."

"I was wondering—"

"Yes, yes, yes."

"I'm just getting into backwa—"

"Malaysia," he answered.

"I'm a backward runner and I'd like to get better and I understand that you're a very accomplished backward runner and so I'd like to learn something about it from you." I said it all as fast and as loud as I could so he couldn't interrupt me again.

There was a crackling silence on the line. I could hear a strange voice in the background, repeating what I had said. Veerabadran coughed and repositioned the phone.

"I accept," he said.

"What?"

"I am honored to be your teacher. When you come to Chennai?"

"Uhh . . ."

"You come to Chennai and we train. Guaranteed you will win."

"Win what?" I said. "I was just kind of hoping to learn a little more about backward running over the phone."

"You need only willpower. Only willpower and guaranteed you will win. We will train. I will be your teacher. When you will come to Chennai?"

"I'm not sure."

"Good, very good. Yes, okay, okay. We will pick you up at the airport."

"I'm not sure—"

"Very good, very good. We will wait for you to call. Thank you, thank you. Bye, bye, bye."

And he hung up.

Over dinner that night, I asked Tara if she had any interest in visiting her family in India.

"No," she said, because she knew where this was heading. "Watching you run backward around the world is not my idea of a vacation."

"We could have a nice time in Italy."

"What's in Italy?" she asked, suspicious.

"The Vatican, the Uffizi, Poviglio."

"Poviglio?"

I took out the atlas and explained that Poviglio was the site of the world's most prestigious backward-running contest. I opened the book to Italy but couldn't find the town on the map.

"Well, I'm sure it's a great place," I said, though I didn't sound so confident. "I mean, come on, it's Italy. It can't be that bad."

"I want pictures." She was tempted by the idea of a vacation in Italy. We'd been saving up some money and plane tickets were cheap at the moment.

I tried to find something on the Web but only turned up shots of people running backward. In the background there were trees, but Tara was unimpressed. She told me that I'd have to carve additional time out of my schedule. She wasn't going to let me hijack our one vacation for some "crazy personal vendetta against nothing," as she referred to it.

But Tara did think that it would be good for me to see Poornima. Poornima could straighten me out, Tara said, and she told me to go if I could find a way of paying for it. Later that night, I found a way. I charged it to our credit card.

I called Veerabadran back and explained that I planned on running the Golden Shrimp and would be honored if he would help me get ready for it. I told him that I could come to India for five or six days before the race if he was open to the idea. I wasn't entirely sure that he understood me, but when he offered again to pick me up at the airport I felt a little better. I told him that my family would pick me up but repeated the date a few times to make sure that he understood when I planned to arrive.

"Guaranteed you will win!" he declared emphatically. I don't think he necessarily meant that I would win the Golden Shrimp—he had been telling me I would win even before I told him I was racing. The way I understood it, he was implying that the training he offered would allow a person to win whatever it is he wanted to win.

But going to India was a risk. First, I could get all the way over there and this guy could have left town for some reason. Despite my efforts to get him to understand that I was coming to see him, it was never clear to me that he fully got it. Plus, he was sixty now and sounded half-crazy. Maybe he was a fantastic backward runner twenty years ago, but the sport had evolved. Maybe there were new techniques, new training regimens that he wasn't familiar with.

But I had a feeling about Veerabadran. In his pictures, he was a little man in gray trousers. He was not built like an athletic superstar. He was just some government-employed dish-towel salesman who had the inner strength to transform his life by running backward. I wanted to learn what he knew.

I sent an e-mail to Paolo telling him that I was going to come to Italy for his race. He sent me back Stefano Morselli's e-mail address, saying that the Golden Shrimp champ spoke better English and would be better able to answer questions about the event. Morselli had been running it every year since 1992, so he knew all the details.

I sent a quick note to Morselli and got back this reply: "You run backward now? YOU RAN EVENTS NEVER? Have you a website? I want to know your details. Ciao Stefano"

I could hear him sneer: "Any backward runner of substance should have a website." But I wasn't going to let the fact that I didn't have one throw me off my game. In fact, his e-mail revealed a lot to me. The champion could sense a threat. He was probably worried that an American contender had come out of the woodwork. And already he was playing mind games (all those silly capital letters), trying to belittle me by implying that I was a novice. Little did he know he was up against an internationally ranked armwrestler and one-time near-professional bullfighter. I wrote him back, telling him that I had never raced backward before but that I was planning on coming to the Golden Shrimp. By letting him know that I was a beginner, I figured he'd underestimate me and wouldn't train as hard. He wasn't the only one who could play mind games.

I began my training in earnest now. Every other day, I scooted over to Kezar Stadium and started to whittle down my times. The difference between backward running and everything else I'd tried was that I am actually a good runner to begin with. Unlike armwrestling, bullfighting, or sumo, I've run since I was in high school. I posted a not-too-shabby three-hour marathon a few years ago. If I was going to excel at anything, this was it.

At first, I ran just one lap as fast as I could. I logged a 2:45 lap, which would bring me in at 19:15 over three kilometers if I kept up that speed. I wasn't discouraged. I knew now what it felt like to cover the full distance, so I could start to better allocate my energy over time.

Running backward on a track was good for me in other ways as well. Since the ground was uniform, I didn't have to worry as much about what was behind me. I was able to simply run, close my eyes if I wanted to, and not worry about the visuals. All that mattered was the movement of my legs.

Sometimes, I'd open my eyes and feel like I was sitting in the back of the old station wagon Mom bought when she gave up on greatness and sold her two-seater sports car. It was a boxy silver Volvo and had a backseat that faced the rear of the car. On long road trips, I'd sit there by myself and watch the world roll out from underneath the car. I felt like an astronaut in a remote-control space pod. Mission control, in the front seat, ran the expedition—all I had to do was sit and observe. Backward running made me an observer in the same way. I felt like someone else was at the controls and I just got to watch as stuff appeared and then drifted away.

I was enjoying my I-don't-care-what's-behind-me jogs until I ran over a fourteen-year-old girl. It was in the early afternoon and a high school PE teacher had brought her kids to the track. They were dejectedly doing laps and for some reason this plump girl was loping along in the fast lane. I was admiring how green the trees were and had spent the previous few minutes looking at a set of thin, wispy clouds. I was barely even aware of the track even though I was posting a 2:30 lap.

When I smacked into her, I didn't know what happened. It had become inconceivable that there was anything behind me. Mission control had failed me. I reached behind to brace myself for the fall and plunged my hand into her ass. She stumbled forward without making a noise, steadied herself, and prevented both of us from hitting the ground.

I apologized profusely. Luckily, neither of us was hurt, though we were both startled and a little confused. But the girl was mostly mortified and had the air of someone who, above all, did not want to be looked at. She turned crimson and anxiously glanced at the other students, who were way ahead of her on the track. The PE teacher jogged over.

"What the hell's wrong with you?" she said to me.

"I'm really sorry," I said. "I wasn't looking where I was going."

"And why would that be?" she said, in the slow, crisp tone I'm sure she used for her discipline cases. It inspired fear and a deep sense of my own obvious stupidity. "Could it be because you were running backward?" This last part pitched up into an aggressive shout.

"Yes, ma'am," I said. "I'm really sorry. I'll just call it a day."

The PE teacher glared at me while the girl stared at the ground. Her classmates had rounded the far end and were heading our way. The PE teacher could tell that it would make the girl feel even worse if the other kids arrived, so she told her to keep running. The girl mumbled an apology and restarted her slow, heavy-footed lope.

I could feel the teacher's eyes burning into my back as I walked off the track. I felt terrible. It seemed to me that the inability to see behind you was the defining weakness of backward running. If I could solve that issue, the sport would be safer. Fewer people would get run over.

The answer seemed simple: a rearview mirror. I had seen bikers wearing small mirrors connected to their eyeglasses, so I stopped by a bike store on my way home and asked the guy behind the counter if he had any clip-on mirrors. He handed me a couple of options and I asked if I could give them a try. He nodded, so I stepped out onto the street in front of the shop and took off backward at a good pace. The clerk came running out from behind the counter and stood on the street to watch me. The look on his face indicated that he thought I was pulling an elaborate theft, but, honestly, who would steal a fifteen-dollar clip-on mirror by running away backward?

Anyway, the mirror was too heavy and immediately slipped down my nose so that I couldn't see anything. It probably worked fine for a biker who didn't move much, but it was useless for a backward runner. I trotted back to the suspicious clerk, who chuckled and said that now he'd seen it all. I would just have to learn to deal with the fact that I didn't know where I was headed.

When I stepped off the plane in Chennai, I felt the suck of wet heat in front of me and the cool, dry airplane air behind me. It was as if I were walking into an elastic barrier between the two. The barrier stretched until I walked too far into the gangway and then it snapped back, banishing the cool and surrounding me with heat.

Arriving in Chennai was like going through a time warp. Suddenly, it was 1982. The gangways were boxy rectangles that would have been a fitting, futuristic backdrop at the unveiling of the DeLorean. The chairs inside the terminal were brown plastic bucket seats and every guard, immigration official, and janitor wore a thick *Magnum, P.I.* mustache.

At the exit, mustachioed taxi drivers swarmed me, jostling one another and offering suggestions about where I might want to go. The beach, temples, yoga center, business center, and Himalayas, three thousand miles away, were all options that I declined.

Poornima arrived a few minutes after I came out. She was draped in a flowing blue sari and patted a handkerchief to her forehead in exasperation before shooing the taxi wallahs away. I hadn't seen her in two years but she hadn't changed.

"You should have told them to stop bothering you," she reprimanded me first off. She has always had an overwhelming goodness about her. She is intensely concerned for her family's well-being, down to the minutest details. If she thought I was upset by a bunch of Tom Selleck look-alikes, it would have been useless arguing. She believed strongly that she knew what was best and, frankly, it was comforting to relinquish control and just nod.

After the taxi drivers scurried away, she gave me a quick once-over, decided that I looked good enough, and ushered me to the car she had rented for the evening. We turned left onto the main road and were instantly surrounded by honking vehicles of every sort. Four cows, two big and two small, trudged heavily across the road. An ancient red, green, yellow, and blue bus, perspiring people out of every opening, swerved around the cows without braking while little yellow three-wheeled motorized rickshaws darted to either side, buzzing like bees on methamphetamine. There were ox-pulled carts affixed with the squeeze horns most often employed by clowns and hundreds of motorcycles whipping through every available parting in the traffic. A single motorcycle sometimes carried a whole family—father driving, wife sitting sidesaddle with a baby in her arms, little girl wedged between Mommy and Daddy, and the adventurous five-year-old son sitting on the handlebars. And Daddy didn't slow down either—he drove just as aggressively as the bus drivers. A dark brown haze of diesel and kerosene smoke enshrouded the noise and movement.

"So you are here to walk backward," Poornima began. I was still trying to cope with the sudden influx of diesel smoke and didn't feel ready to defend myself.

"Is this a very popular activity in America?" she asked, in a tone that implied that Americans were crazy anyway, so it wouldn't surprise her.

She looked at me expectantly. This was my turn to explain what I was doing with my life, so I laid it all out. I explained that I had been trying out a bunch of different things, from bullfighting to temp work. After my armwrestling and bullfighting experiences, I felt a lot more confident and started to make a living as a writer. Now I had a steady writing gig but still felt something was missing from my life. It was a sense of direction. I wasn't sure where I was headed and it made me anxious and unhappy.

Backward running was helping me accustom myself to the fact that I didn't know what was ahead. My old reaction would have been to slow down and worry. My new sport was teaching me to move fast and comfortably, despite my doubts. I didn't know what the next step would bring but I was learning to accept whatever it was and adapt. I was becoming more at ease with life.

Poornima looked at me blankly. I was starting to sound like Christian Grollé. I could tell she was thinking her niece had married a madman. The question was, what could she do about it? I was obviously not pursuing a standard job track. It wasn't accounting or software programming, both of which were very sensible occupations. Could I really be expected to support Tara and a family over the years? Maybe it was working now, but what about in five years? Children are not fed by wild antics and incomprehensible speeches about the spirituality of backward running.

On the other hand, America was a strange place. She had watched *Dallas*. She knew that people in America did not have to do a lot to make money. Maybe I was a normal American. She hadn't met many other Americans in person so she didn't have a solid basis for comparison.

I could sense this thought process tilting slightly in my favor, so I added that the magazine had even signed a contract with me. Contracts are things that accountants and software engineers have.

"There's all these books and magazines in the world," I said. "Somebody has to write all that stuff. And it's not like people are all of a sudden going to stop reading. They probably won't stop reading for another thirty or forty years. That's plenty of time to have kids, raise a family, and have a nice life."

Poornima nodded cautiously. She patted her forehead with the handkerchief and changed the subject to the drought that was affecting the city. I had convinced her! Or, at least, I had done enough to make her think that I didn't need immediate straightening out. It was a relief.

Still, I was coursing with nervousness. I had overcome one hurdle but now had to contend with the fact that I had flown all the way around the world to meet a man with whom I'd spoken twice and who may or may not have understood English. I imagined calling him from Poornima's phone and getting no answer. I would look for him at his shop, but, according to Poornima, he was retired and didn't go there anymore. I could already see Poornima's eyes rolling—the same annoyed look Tara often gave me. Why did I spend hard-earned money to go chase some half-assed dream across three continents?

But that was the whole point. I was running backward, literally and figuratively. I didn't know what was going to happen next because I didn't have eyes in the back of my head. In other words, I wasn't going to let the fact that I didn't know how this was going to turn out prevent me from achieving my goals. I wanted to run backward at a world-class pace and I wanted to be comfortable with the fact that it was scary.

Poornima's house was a two-level building with four rooms, though her whole family slept on two beds in one of the rooms. There were her teenage son and daughter, her sister Padmini (another of Tara's aunts), and her sister-in-law Uma, who was in her late sixties. Uma had two teeth and glowed with warmth despite being on the verge of death due to a heart condition. I was dispatched to the upstairs room, which was spacious and had the only air conditioner. Poornima spent ten minutes trying to convince me to turn on the machine, but I steadfastly refused. I wanted to face the heat head-on, like everyone else.

I dropped my bags upstairs, deflected a number of demands to eat mango, and dialed Veerabadran's number from Poornima's phone. I gripped the handset tightly as the rings sounded out. And then Veerabadran picked up.

"Yes, hello!" he shouted.

In a country of a billion people, it seemed like more than coincidence that Veerabadran lived near Poornima. India is the second most populated country on the planet, and Chennai, with it's 3.5 million people, is India's third largest city. It is a city overflowing with people. They sleep on the streets, beside fetid rivers, and pour out of crumbling concrete buildings tinted green from the humidity. And yet somehow it turned out that Veerabadran's house was just ten blocks away.

If Bombay is the New York of India, then Chennai is its Los Angeles. It's a low-rise, spread-out city that would take at least two hours of hard work to navigate in a car. It was a blessing that Veerabadran lived so close. It took Chetan, Poornima's eighteen-year-old son, less than five minutes to drive me over on his motorcycle.

The houses in the neighborhood were all two or three stories and looked very nice by Indian standards. That is to say that they weren't in an advanced stage of deterioration and didn't look like they were built one brick at a time over a period of thirty years.

I asked Chetan what he knew about Veerabadran's street. Was this still a good neighborhood? Chetan wobbled his head—a classic Indian gesture that is somewhere between yes and no. Generally, the head wobble means "I hear the words that are coming out of your mouth." I got the sense that there was something he wasn't telling me.

Veerabadran was standing outside, waiting. He looked just like he did in his pictures: he stood five feet four inches, had skin the color of dark-stained mahogany, and wore trousers and a button-down shirt. The main difference was that now he was smiling broadly.

"Mr. George," he said, taking my hand and not letting go. He couldn't pronounce Joshua so he'd decided to call me George. "Very big pleasure. Much pleasure."

He was actually speaking softly—the shouting must have been a phone thing—but he kept shaking my hand, nodding his head, and patting me on the back. Chetan left hurriedly and Veerabadran introduced me to his son Prem without letting go of my hand. I finally had to yank it away to shake Prem's hand. Prem was my height, preppily dressed, and seemed a world apart from his father, though he clearly deferred to him.

Veerabadran had leased the bottom of his three-story home to a spice-exporting business and an engineer rented the top. His family lived in four small rooms on the middle floor. When we walked up, I met Babu, his younger son, and Mrs. Veerabadran, his pretty but frail wife. Some beefy young guy, a friend of Babu's, documented my arrival with a digital camera. Everybody was well dressed and I realized that meeting me was a big deal for them.

We sat on a thinly cushioned wooden couch and the group looked at me with anticipation. I sensed that I was expected to make a speech so I cleared my throat and started speaking about the first thing that came to mind. I told them about the Golden Shrimp and then said that I was here to learn from the master. At that, Veerabadran patted my knee.

"Very jolly. Very jolly," he said. "You will win."

While I was talking, Veerabadran periodically looked at Prem and Prem quietly translated pieces of what I was saying. The old man spoke some English but was far from fluent. He said something to Prem, who asked if I was married. When I told them I was, Veerabadran looked very pleased.

"Wife is very important," he said. "Without my wife, I would not be. Wife is cornerstone."

His wife smiled shyly and left the room to get me a cup of tea. Veerabadran explained that when he decided, at the age of forty, to challenge the backward-running world record, everybody in the family except his wife was against it. Relatives came over to try to talk him out of it. They said it was foolish and had no purpose. They said he would hurt himself. And it would be expensive. He would have to hire umpires to legitimize it, buy new shoes, and pay for food to be hospitable to the friends and family who came to watch him. Since he planned on setting the record on a track, he would also have to hire a stadium for twenty-four hours. All of this was expensive for a man who was making two hundred dollars a month. *"Where did he think he was going to get the money?"* everyone wanted to know.

He dismissed his critics but had no good answers to their questions. Then, one morning, his wife came to him wiping away tears and gave him a shoe box. The box contained all her gold jewelry; her father had given it to her before she married Veerabadran. It represented all her independent wealth in the world. She told him to take it to a loan shark. He could use it as collateral to raise the necessary money.

When she came back with my tea, she told me, through Prem, that she didn't understand why her husband felt so strongly about walking backward. "I thought he was a crazy man to get this idea at the age of forty," she said. But it didn't matter to her because she could see it was important to him. More than that, she said, she knew it was critical for his well-being.

Veerabadran was staring at his wife with passion. I coughed and he looked back at me.

"Very good woman," he said, almost breathless. "Very, very. She is queen."

"What happened to the jewelry?" I asked.

"I received promotion," Veerabadran said. "Three promotions because I am Guinness record holder. With extra money from promotion, I buy back jewelry."

"What gold I gave my husband is now worth many times its weight in honor," his wife said.

"Back running made my father a very important man," Prem added matter-of-factly. "It changed all our lives."

As proof, Prem handed me a thick sheaf of papers. It was a twenty-five-page spreadsheet detailing the names, skin complexions, education, and professions of hundreds of young men and women looking to get married. They all had come to Veerabadran asking him to help them find a mate. Indians traditionally have arranged marriages so they have a lot of confidence in their matchmakers. It showed that the community held Veerabadran in high regard.

There was also a steady stream of supplicants who came to his house to ask advice, on everything from building a new community center to how to break the world record for distance roller skating.

"There is a boy," Veerabadran said. "He is sixteen. He will roller-skate one hundred kilometers in five hours. I am helping him. He is good boy."

In addition to the boy, Veerabadran had coached and certified numerous other record holders. There was the man who sang nonstop for thirty-seven hours, another guy who rode a bicycle one-handed from one end of India to the other (he was holding an Indian flag in the other hand), and an artist who drew continuously for sixteen hours without lifting his pen.

"These people, they want to achieve something," Veerabadran told me. "Also, they were unemployed."

"There are a lot of people in India," Prem said. "You have to find some way to distinguish yourself. Being record holders helped them stand out from the rest and get jobs. And it made them more confident in their lives."

I asked Veerabadran if he was just coaching now and he stood up and shook his finger in the air over his head.

"I am always record holder," he said forcefully. "I welcome all challenge. If another makes new record, very, very good. Maybe you make new record. I am happy only. Only happy. But also, I am ready to set new new record. I am not lazy man."

Veerabadran's words were oddly familiar to me. I suddenly felt as if I had met him a long time ago. As I watched him speak, I could hear an echo coming back to me from my childhood: I was five, lying in my bed. My dad raised his finger into the air and Ipski-Pipski spoke through him, announcing that he welcomed all challengers to his Indy 500 record. And then, with a glint in his eye, Ipski-Pipski declared that he had invented yet another challenge for himself. The story would have to be continued another night.

Well, this, right now, was the continuation. Veerabadran was Ipski-Pipski. He was familiar to me because I had spent my youth imagining him. My childhood idol had been reincarnated as a short Indian man.

I felt goose bumps as Veerabadran declared that he had a grand new undertaking afoot. He planned to set a new world record for nonstop floating. In November, he would rent the local municipal swimming pool for three days and attempt to float on his back with no buoyancy devices for seventy-four hours. Why, having already accomplished so much, would he do such a thing?

"Just to have some thrill in life," he said, as only Ipski-Pipski could.

I woke up at 4:15 the next morning at Poornima's. It was dark out and the mosquitoes buzzed languidly on the other side of the room. They were drunk on my blood and could barely stay aloft. The room was a cool 90 degrees. By ten, it would be pushing 100 outside. Veerabadran said that we needed to meet at 5:00 in order to train without getting heatstroke.

I walked to his house on the empty streets. The road I followed was paralleled by a ten-foot-wide putrid stream that even from a distance made me nauseous. It threw off the scent of flame-broiled feces and black licorice. Trucks and rickshaws parked beside it. The drivers slept soundly on the flatbeds. Some even slept in the dirt bank by the miasma.

Veerabadran was waiting for me when I got to his house. "Did you brush teeth?" he asked through the darkness.

"Yes," I replied, confused.

"Ahh," he said and waved me up to the roof. He was barefoot and there was a pile of shoes on the landing, so I left my shoes and followed him up the stairs. On the way up, I asked him why he was interested in my teeth. He nodded his head and said, "Yes."

The rough tiled roof was illuminated by dim predawn light. Veerabadran started jogging sleepily in tight concentric circles. The area was only about thirty feet by twenty feet and was haphazardly lined with stacked planks of wood. It didn't seem wise to be jogging barefoot in the dark on a tiny roof littered with construction material, but Veerabadran wasn't concerned. He focused on pinching his nose and breathing out of only one nostril at a time.

"You take," he said, motioning at my nose as we spun around and around. The diameter of the circle between us was no more than fifteen feet, and it took about ten seconds to complete a lap. Veerabadran demonstrated how I was supposed to breathe in through one nostril, hold it as long as I could, and let it out through the other nostril, then repeat in the reverse.

"Very good yoga," he said. "Very strong."

I suspected that it was an elaborate nose-picking ruse as I saw Veerabadran fling a booger off his finger. Still, I did what he told me. I didn't want to appear unworthy at my first training session. But after a dozen silent laps and innumerable nostril-flaring inhalations, my bare feet were rubbing painfully on the tiles. I had no idea how long he planned on doing this. Was it best to stop and put on my shoes? I thought we were going to go running on the streets.

But if Veerabadran was going to do it barefoot, I resolved to do it, too. He spun and started trotting backward, so I followed suit. A bird squawked. I looked up and, like a kid in the back of the station wagon again, I noticed the violet-blue sky and ramshackle neighborhood roofs in the gathering light. A crescent moon hovered over the palm-dotted horizon. It suddenly seemed very funny to me. I was running in circles, backward and barefoot, on a roof in India at five in the morning. I laughed and felt better for about five minutes.

Of course, the humor of the situation faded with every lap. After thirty minutes, my ankles were swelling and the skin was rubbing off my feet. But I had entered a rare mental state. The running became so repetitive that even the pain seemed common and somehow numbing. There was definitely part of me screaming for a stop to this madness, but as we kept going round and round, the screaming eventually became a bore and was easier to ignore.

Veerabadran peered at me and periodically mumbled enigmatic exhortations like "Yes, yes" and "Happily, happily." After forty-five minutes of running, he said, "Ten minutes more." A half hour later, he announced that we only had five minutes left. To get to four minutes left took ten minutes. Every minute in Veerabadran's world counted for five after that.

Finally, it was over. I sat down and bent over to examine my battered feet but Veerabadran bustled down the stairs.

"Headstanding, headstanding," he said, trailing away. I reluctantly and painfully pushed myself up again and limped downstairs to find Veerabadran standing on his head in his living room. He watched me watch him for a moment and then dropped down.

"Five minutes," he said. He had a pillow laid out against the wall. "Five minutes only."

He pointed at the pillow. "You," he said. "Courage, courage."

I placed my head on the pillow and kicked my feet into the air, resting them on the wall for balance. The blood rushed out of my feet and into my head, threatening to explode out of my ears. But the numbness that had been with me on the roof persisted and I once again felt comfortable and calm despite now being upside down. The five minutes—if that's what it was—went by in a flash. I was now in Veerabadran's world.

"My father is the only man who has gone backward in order to go forward in life," Prem told me at lunch later that day. Veerabadran had left for a meeting with a politician so Prem took me out on the town for a couple of hours. "Without backward running, we wouldn't be eating here."

The restaurant was a big cafeteria-style hall with a fleet of waiters wearing little white caps. Prem told me that it was a famous, highly respected establishment in Chennai, but it looked like a soup kitchen at a homeless shelter. The waiters carried around large metal pails filled with food. A huge banana leaf was laid out in front of me and one of the waiters ladled a pile of soupy brown slop onto the leaf. Another dropped a dollop of rice and a third spatted down a tablespoon of chutney.

"I will be honest with you," Prem said. "We are from the backward caste. We are what was known as the Untouchables."

He looked at me with a fiery pride. I could tell that it was hard for him to say this. The Indian caste system has been around for more than a thousand years and for most of the time it has been used to oppress the people at the bottom. There are roughly five levels in the system. The Brahmins, at the top, have traditionally ruled India. The warrior class is next down, followed by the merchants and the farmers. The Untouchables are so excluded that they aren't even considered to be a rung on the ladder: they are simply not a part of society except for the fact that they are expected to sweep the streets and clean the toilets of the higher castes.

They are particularly reviled by Brahmins, who refer to them as the backward caste and historically have prohibited them from living anywhere near Brahmin communities. Brahmins consider them so physically and spiritually polluted that if a member of the backward caste touches one of them, the Brahmin has to be ritually cleansed by a priest. Tara's family are Brahmins, which might explain Chetan's uneasiness when he first dropped me off at Veerabadran's house.

Mahatma Gandhi devoted a lot of energy to elevating the lower castes. He called the Untouchables "Harijan," which means "children of God," and supported a massive affirmative action campaign that continues to this day. There are now reserved seats in universities and Parliament for the "scheduled caste"—as in, they are scheduled for something better.

But the discrimination persists. "The truth," Prem said, "is that my father was not getting promoted at his work. Even though it was a government textile agency, still they did not promote him. He was forty years old. He was an ambitious man but was being passed over because he was from the backward caste."

Veerabadran's parents were impoverished farmers in the countryside. He grew up in a mud hut with four siblings, all of whom dropped out of school by the eighth grade to work on the farm. Veerabadran was different—he didn't think it was right that his family worked so hard and still didn't have enough to eat. The family recognized Veerabadran's drive and agreed to let him continue his studies. He was the first person in his family to graduate from high school. He went on to college, and at the time he took the textile job, his future seemed bright.

But, almost twenty years later, nothing in his life had changed. He was still in the same entry-level position, even though he was a hard worker and felt more competent than others of higher castes who had long ago ascended the management ladder. He sank into a depression and for the first time felt weary. He was losing himself. It was as if the person he had been were disappearing, only to be replaced by a short, bitter, dark-skinned Untouchable. He began to think of himself the way Brahmins thought of him.

And then he read a newspaper article about an American who had run backward eighty-one miles in twenty-four hours and set a Guinness World Record. Veerabadran immediately recognized the opportunity: Americans were even higher up the social ladder than Brahmins. If he could beat the American record, he would demonstrate to the world that he was not just some lowly Untouchable who didn't deserve to be promoted. He would be ranked above an American. And he would do it in a way that made a strength of what others felt to be his weakness: his backward status.

It was a tantalizing, almost feverishly exciting plan and it opened up the possibilities of life again. He no longer felt trapped and tired. As a farm boy, he had run everywhere, usually barefoot. If there was one thing he knew, it was how to run. Maybe he couldn't beat a Brahmin on a science examination or on the cricket pitch, but he was sure he could retrorun the pants off any man, American, Brahmin, or otherwise.

Later, at his house, I saw a water-stained photo of him at this time. He was standing on a small podium with his right index finger pointed emphatically to the sky. A microphone stood in front of him. This was the moment when he announced that he was going to break the American-held twenty-four-hour continuous backward-running record. His body arched like a bow toward an unseen (nonexistent?) crowd and a slight potbelly slipped over his belt. Even in its deteriorated state, the picture conveyed his absolute, undeniable conviction. The motivated, optimistic Veerabadran was back and people were going to have to take him seriously.

I arrived at five in the morning again for my next training session. The air felt relatively crisp and fresh, though it was already pushing 90 degrees. My feet were still sore and raw from yesterday, but I had glimpsed a way to shut off the pain. Veerabadran didn't talk a lot but he knew exactly what he was doing. Running backward at high speed for two miles is all about pain. You've got to be able to increase your pain threshold in order to decrease your time. Veerabadran was quietly giving me a unique set of mental tools.

Today, though, he put on a pair of surprisingly hip-looking running shoes and jumped on a bus.

"Beach, beach," he said.

The beach in Chennai is bordered on one side by the mammoth cranes and bulk-freight tankers of the port of Chennai. At the other end—about a mile away—the sand abruptly turns into an endless shantytown. In between these two bookends is what appeared to be a nice, wide beach. The bus dropped us off and Veerabadran led the way onto the sand.

The shoreline was crowded with fishermen casting lines directly into the surf. The sun hadn't yet crested the horizon but there was a nice pale-blue light in the sky. We watched one guy pull in a line of five gasping catfish and Veerabadran got excited. He poked one of the fish until the fisherman shouted at him. Fish was an unusual luxury for Veerabadran. It was expensive and he almost never ate it. So Veerabadran disregarded the fisherman's standoffishness and asked how much for all five fish. The price was thirty rupees (about seventy cents). Veerabadran whispered to me that it was a very good price and handed the fisherman a few dirty bills.

A minute later, I had five still-wiggling catfish strapped to the outside of my backpack. They were wrapped in a thin plastic bag but the bag was full of holes, so fish juice dribbled out of the bag and streamed down my legs.

"Now we run backward," Veerabadran said.

We set off at a slow backward trot and almost immediately passed a man taking a shit at the high-tide line. We ran within ten feet of him but he didn't seem to mind. In fact, he watched us from his squatting position with a bewildered look. Clearly, we were the strange ones. A hundred yards farther, we passed another guy taking a shit. I started to notice intermittent piles of feces. I realized abruptly that the beach doubled as a latrine for the shantytown residents and fishermen of the area.

This was problematic. I couldn't see the piles coming since I was running backward. A great sense of relief would pass over me every time one would appear off to my left or right. It meant that I hadn't stepped in it. It was like running blindfolded through a minefield.

It also made me reconsider the fish strapped to my back. They had been caught bottom-feeding just off the shore. Basically, they were shit-eating fish. Veerabadran planned to cook them for lunch today and I was going to have a hard time saying I didn't want any.

Veerabadran didn't seem to mind the shit. He just kept running and eventually the odds turned against us. After a half mile, my new Asics running shoes were streaked with feces and I just stopped caring. What was I going to do? I couldn't look over my shoulder constantly and plot out the minefield. The shits were pale brown and hard to see against the sand. The best I could do was avoid the steady line of guys who had come down to the shore to squat.

Once again, Veerabadran had succeeded in building up a mental state conducive to backward running. I couldn't think of anything worse than running backward through a field of shit with a bunch of shit-eating fish strapped to my back. But if I could handle that, then I could definitely handle Italy's clean streets.

Veerabadran stopped when we passed a well-dressed husband and wife who were burying their two children in the sand. As usual, we hadn't seen them coming, and the sight was so arresting, our backward movement just petered out. The kids were sunk up to their chests and were just about eye-level with the waves rushing up the beach. When the tide turned, they would surely be drowned. The younger of the two was screaming while the older looked brave and angelic. The husband rested on his shovel and the sari-clad wife watched silently.

"Madam, what do you do?" Veerabadran asked the lady. He was more curious than concerned.

"It's for their legs," she said in clear English. "I was watching you. Why are you running backward?"

Veerabadran looked at me, momentarily overwhelmed by her fluent English. She had the light skin and sense of superiority common to Brahmins.

"I'm training," I said curtly, matching her elliptical response with my own. She was accusing us of acting strange. "Listen, lady," I wanted to say, "I'm not the one burying my kids at the high-tide line." But rather than getting overly aggressive, I asked what the burying had to do with their legs.

She explained that she and her husband were originally from Chennai but currently ran a software business in Cincinnati, Ohio. While in the United States, her children had developed bowlegs. I couldn't see the kids' legs, so I couldn't assess the extent of the bow, but I'd never heard of anyone besides cowboys having bowlegs. Either way, she wanted her kids' legs to be perfectly straight, so she went to various orthopedic specialists in the United States who basically told her that there was nothing wrong with her kids.

But she continued to notice what she thought of as an intolerable curve of the leg. So, a month ago, when they came back to Chennai to visit their families for a summer vacation, an old aunt described to them the traditional cure. It involved burying children in the sand at the ocean's edge for an hour before sunrise every day for two weeks. The mother speculated that the children's bones might be more flexible early in the morning and that the weight of the wet sand by the shore would push their little legs straight.

She spoke as if it were a networking problem and these measures were part of a reasonable hardware remedy. Seeing the look on my face, she could sense that it sounded crazy, and maybe part of her believed that it was. But here she was, with her two children buried in the beach. She was defiant, embarrassed, and hopeful that it would work. After all, this was just the beginning of the second week of daily burying.

As we jogged away backward, we had plenty of time to watch them. The two kids stared into the waves and the parents watched us. At that moment, I felt a lot like those kids. I was buried up to my neck in a training regimen meant to reshape my legs. Fortunately, I wasn't eye-level with feces-laden waves. But being five feet above it all wasn't much consolation. I wasn't in as bad a situation as those kids, but I wasn't doing too well for myself either.

We moved into the soft sand farther away from the waves and I noticed a man racing toward us, flapping his arms. He had a big smile, so I didn't think he was warning us about something. When Veerabadran spotted him, he shouted. This was Mr. Panja, a friend of his, who had come to the beach to meet us. Veerabadran introduced him as the man who would soon break the headstand record. Panja was building up to a four-hour headstand, beating the old record of one hour. Though this shit-saturated beach was not the ideal place to be doing headstands, Panja immediately bent over and kicked his feet into the air. I thought it was just a little show-and-tell, but he didn't come down, nor was he able to talk. Veerabadran and I waited silently as a light wind whipped sand into the guy's inverted face. He spit out the sand but still didn't come down.

"Is he going for the record right now?" I asked after a minute of awkwardly standing there.

"No, no, no," Veerabadran said and tapped Panja on the leg. The man came down, brushed the sand off his arms, and we resumed the introductions as if he hadn't just stood on his head for sixty seconds.

Panja was younger than Veerabadran. He had inky black hair and a mustache to match. I asked him if he lived around here and he said no. He lived forty minutes away. It seemed odd that he would come all the way out here at six in the morning just to demonstrate his headstand for me. I could sense that there was a plan afoot.

"You will have breakfast with Panja," Veerabadran declared. He said that Panja would drive me on his motorcycle.

I protested. I didn't want to spend forty minutes on the back of Panja's motorcycle at the beginning of rush hour in Chennai. It was bad enough in a car or bus. I had images of us getting into a wreck and I started to feel panicky. I didn't want to go with this guy. With all that headstanding, he could have a stroke at any second.

I phrased my objections as tactfully as I could. I said I was tired, I had gotten up so early, and I had already eaten at Poornima's house. Veerabadran wasn't having it. He just kept repeating the word *good* as he backed down the beach and disappeared around a thatched shanty.

I was abandoned with Panja, so I got on the motorcycle and we sped off into the traffic.

Panja was a Christian. I realized this when I walked into his simple living room. One wall was covered with high-resolution wallpaper that depicted an enticing tropical beach. The other wall was taken up with a six-foot-tall billboard that said JESUS: SAVIOR,

HEALER, BAPTIZER, COMING KING. The hand-painted lettering was made to look like fire.

A plump, pretty girl in her late teens came out dressed in a *salwar kameez*, a traditional pants-and-tunic combination. Panja introduced her as his daughter Sita. When his equally plump wife appeared, Panja led me into a low-ceilinged, windowless space between the tropical Jesus room and the propane-powered Indian kitchen. We sat at a small circular table and the women brought out food. Panja scarfed his down, insisted I take my time, and left the room. The wife disappeared as well. I was left with the daughter, who brought out another platter of small rice pancakes and sat down next to me.

The daughter smiled flirtatiously and asked me about my life in America. I got the sense I was being courted. Maybe Veerabadran was trying to work some of his matchmaking magic. After all, it's not every day that an American Christian boy shows up in town. I tried to prevent any false hopes by saying, in passing, that I was married.

When I mentioned my marital status, she pointed at a black-and-white photograph standing on a corner table. The picture showed a dapper Indian man flanked by two long-skirted white women who held his arms possessively.

"My grandfather was a ladies' man," Sita said admiringly. "When he went to Italy to fight with the Indian army during the Second World War, he met two sisters who wanted to marry him."

Sita stood up and brought the picture to me so I could take a better look at her grandfather and his two would-be wives.

"They were very fierce with him and wouldn't let him leave. My grandmother was very upset."

"I could see how that would be a problem," I said. I didn't know where to begin. There were a lot of questions that this brought up, not the least of which was the relevance this had to my marital status.

"Was he romantically involved with both of the sisters?" I started.

"They both wanted him so they decided to share him," she said.

"They were very rich so they bought him anything he wanted. He was a very handsome man."

Eventually, after living with these two women for six months, Sita's grandfather convinced his two benefactors to let him return to India so that he could arrange his family affairs before returning to Italy to marry them both. According to Sita, he had intended to go back to Italy, but after his return his Indian wife burned all letters with an Italian postmark. Maybe she burned his return ticket.

Either way, as far as I could see, the house contained no picture of Grandma and Grandpa lovingly gazing into each other's eyes. And, judging by Sita's proud and unabashed display of her grandfather's two-timing, polygamy wasn't out of the question.

And, to be honest, I did suddenly see a happy dual life stretch before me. I liked Sita. I liked her plumpness, her quick smile, and the way she watched me intently as I ate to make sure I was enjoying every bite. But I had a wife already and a good one at that. Veerabadran was working his magic just a little too late.

After breakfast, Panja reappeared, and I asked him to take me back to my aunt's house. Sita said it was too bad I didn't have more time in Chennai and blushed when I shook her hand. She was still watching me when I rounded the corner at the end of the block on the back of her dad's motorcycle.

Veerabadran called me at Poornima's at noon and invited me over for lunch. He said Prem was going to cook something special for me. If it was the fish we had bought that morning, I figured he would have mentioned that. All I wanted to do now was avoid the fish, and it occurred to me that if I ate lunch with them, I could beg off dinner and let them eat their fish then.

I started to walk over, but it was a grueling hike under the midday sun. The open sewer on the right side of the road was festering and bubbling in the heat and sent off a smell so penetrating I tried not to breathe. By the time I arrived, I had no appetite.

When I walked through the doorway, I saw that Prem had already laid out lunch on the marble floor. Worse still, the largest plate was piled high with deep-fried fish.

"What's the matter?" Prem said when he came out of the kitchen and saw me standing on the threshold of the apartment. "You look hot. Please sit down. My father trained you too much this morning and now it's very hot out. Please sit and have some fish. It will make you feel better."

He took me by the arm and sat me on a cushion in front of the shitfish. I could see through a partially open door to Veerabadran's bedroom—the old man was standing on his head and staring blankly at me as if he didn't know me.

"My father is resting," Prem said, following my gaze. "He will be out momentarily."

Prem brought me a glass of water and Veerabadran emerged from his room. He sat down next to me and unceremoniously began eating while Prem brought in plates and chutneys. With his right hand, Veerabadran grabbed a chunk of fish and put it on my plate. He took one for himself, mushed it into some rice and chutney, and popped it into his mouth.

"Very good fish," he said. "Eat, eat."

I pushed the fish around the plate and ate some rice, but Prem came back in and asked me if there was something wrong with the fish. I told him it was excellent fish and pushed it around the plate again. He didn't move. Both of them watched me. I realized I was going to have to eat the damn thing. I tried to think of it as something else, anything else. A vegetable, maybe. I lifted it to my mouth, took a bite, and heard the crashing of waves. Before the image could grow, I gulped down the entire thing, trying not to linger over the taste.

"Yes," Veerabadran said. "This fish will make you very strong indeed."

I distracted myself by immediately praising Prem's cooking. He seemed satisfied and returned to the kitchen while Veerabadran, to my relief, devoured what was left of the fish.

"Tomorrow," he said, "we go back to beach and maybe buy more good fish."

The next morning, before dawn, we did go back to the beach. I offered to pay for a taxi—it would have cost three dollars instead of twenty-five cents on the bus—not a big deal. But Veerabadran was adamant. He always took the cheapest option.

"I am a simple man," he said. "Why do I need taxi?"

He grabbed my hand and led me aboard a bus, which was empty at this early hour.

"I am come from small village," he said solemnly. "But there is meaning in my life. I will tell you."

Holding his hand made me feel like his grandson. He was about as different from my actual grandfather as you could get, but, after only a few days together, he already treated me like a member of his fam-

Joshua Davis

ily. I could feel a warmth between us. It was as if I had passed a series of tacit tests and was now fully accepted.

"Many, many girls want me because I am Guinness record
holder," he said as the driver accelerated rapidly down the empty
predawn streets. Veerabadran braced himself against me, afraid of
being knocked over. His body felt fragile, like he might break a bone
if jostled too hard. I held him up and laughed. It was funny that this
short, old man considered himself a sex symbol.

"So many beautiful ladies like me," he said, emphasizing his
point with a wobble of his head. "But I am married man so I say
thank you, thank you, and never, never. This is first principle: no
women. Only wife. She is life partner. She is brilliant lady. I think
only of her."

Veerabadran's first principle was something I needed to hear. Like
Veerabadran's wife, Tara had supported me when I most needed it.
She paid the bills for four years while I tried to find a way to make a
living that didn't involve data entry at the phone company. I was
here in India learning how to be the best backward runner in the
world because of her support. But because she's so much a part of my
life, I tended not to think about how she was the foundation of my
incipient success in life. I would forget that most people aren't given
as many chances to fail.

Since we met when we were young, the fundamental image Tara
had of me was that of a confident, promising sixteen-year-old boy
who thought he could and would succeed at everything. And though
I had never lived up to that, I still felt her optimism at my core. Tara
loved me like she loved me when we first met. Being married to
someone like her is a rare gift and Veerabadran was right to remind
me of it.

"Second principle: no money," he continued. "Money is corrup-
tion. If you think money and no family, you lose life."

Once again, his words rang true. Now that I was actually making
money, I could feel myself drawn toward my newfound ability to
generate income. Over the course of the year, I had taken on more

work than I could handle and the stress of that was causing me to lose interest in my job. Just calling it a job was a bad sign. Following my curiosity had never been work before. It didn't seem like a very healthy mind-set and I resolved to cut back and learn to live with less. I'd done it before so I could certainly do it again.

"Third principle: everyone make meaning. That is what you must do. You make your own meaning."

He squeezed my hand and his eyes twinkled.

"But I know already," he said. "You will win!"

We arrived on the beach as the sun was rising over the ocean and Veerabadran immediately set out at a fast backward trot.

"When you were setting your twenty-four-hour backward-running record," I asked, "what were you thinking about? Did you have a list of things mapped out to keep your mind occupied?"

"I had only one thought," he said. "I thought of my wife. I meditate on her. She is my meaning."

So I tried it as we entered the Shit Zone. Yesterday, I had gotten to a place where I didn't necessarily care about running through human feces, but today I went a step further. I thought about Tara and how nice it was to lie in bed with her at the end of a day. Just lying there on our sides with her back against my chest. It made me happy. Even after my right foot landed squarely in a pile of yellowish crap, I was smiling.

Twenty hours of travel on planes and trains brought me here, to the front seat of a platypus-esque car heading out of Parma, Italy. Gianpietro, the man driving, didn't speak English very well and haltingly explained that he worked for a sprinkler manufacturer that sponsored the Golden Shrimp. He had picked me up at the train station and was now driving me to my hotel in Poviglio.

Gianpietro seemed reluctant to talk to me, maybe because his

English was limited. But he was the first person I had met so far in Italy, and I was brimming with questions about the race. Ignoring his sullen demeanor, I asked if he was a retrorunner.

"I no run backward," he said, in a tone that implied he was above doing such a thing.

"Are there a lot of backward runners here in Italy?"

"No," he said, keeping his eyes on the road.

"But it's popular?" I asked, suddenly feeling like I'd staked months of my life on something that nobody here actually cared about. "I mean, there are a lot of spectators?"

"No," he said curtly again. "The race is at six so no so many are there."

"It's at six in the morning?"

"Yes."

"Why is it at six in the morning?"

"I no know," he said, obviously not wanting to be helpful. I got the distinct impression that his boss had forced him to pick me up because he hadn't sold enough sprinklers that month.

We sat in silence for a while. It's one thing to hold a marathon at six in the morning—a race that long can last five hours and you don't want to run in the heat. But the Golden Shrimp is only two miles and shouldn't take more than twenty-five minutes for even the slowest person. Maybe they're trying to avoid traffic, but, judging from what I was seeing out the window (fields of wheat and country roads), that didn't seem to be much of a problem.

Maybe it shouldn't have mattered to me when the race was held. I mean, wasn't it all about challenging myself and trying to focus on the good things? This was just the first hurdle.

"So, is Poviglio a nice town?" I asked, changing the subject and focusing on something good.

"No," Gianpietro said bitterly.

"It's not famous for anything like cheese or wine or . . ." I asked, trailing off miserably.

"Absolutely not."

Okay, then. This was going to be great.

Gianpietro dropped me at the quiet Hotel La Sonrisa alongside a country road with vague assurances that I was in the town of Poviglio and that Paolo Pessina would eventually contact me.

Salvatore, the kindly middle-aged guy behind the counter at the hotel, was slightly more encouraging. He told me that this was indeed the right place and that the Golden Shrimp was held on the road that ran alongside the hotel. Sal's English wasn't very good either, but he had a lot more energy. He was particularly impressed that I had come from America to run the race.

But Sal confirmed that it was not a big spectator sport in town. It just seemed a little strange to everyone. Plus, he said there were only about fifteen contestants last year. Still, he welcomed me cheerfully and showed me upstairs to my room, which looked like a narrow closet. It had a single bed that just barely fit and a window that looked out onto the road. I thanked him and lay down dejectedly. I was probably the only person ever to have flown from Chennai, India, to Poviglio, Italy. Now I was seriously doubting the trip had been worthwhile.

An obnoxiously loud phone ring woke me. It was Paolo and he was in the lobby. I had decided to bury my depression by sleeping and now groggily walked downstairs. It was dark out and the hotel's restaurant was unaccountably busy for such a remote place. It had seemed so sleepy only a couple of hours ago.

Paolo hovered nervously in the entryway. He was a compact, sinewy man whose baldness drew attention to the zigzagging veins bulging out of the side of his head. He appeared to have had one too many espressos. Next to him stood a good-looking middle-aged woman. She was dressed in pink hot pants and a skintight, low-cut top that revealed the billowing curve of her breasts. Her eye shadow was a vivid blue and she wore a heart-shaped rhinestone pendant that dangled down into her cleavage. She was startlingly out of place here in the country and even more so alongside Paolo, who wore sandals, shorts, and a gray T-shirt.

I stuck out my hand to greet him. As we shook, he leaned in as if to hug me. Instinctively, I gave him the classic American male response to hugging: the one-handed pat on the back with a little chest thump. He was, in keeping with traditional Italian greetings, actually trying to kiss my cheeks, which he succeeded in doing after he bounced off my chest. But he was clearly confused by the solid thumping I'd just given him on the back.

Nonetheless, he introduced me to his wife, the lady by his side. She smiled weakly in my direction and kept her distance, indicating that I shouldn't expect to kiss her cheeks after the odd and somewhat violent encounter I'd just had with her husband.

Recovering quickly from the awkward introductions, Paolo invited me to dinner at his house, which was only a few hundred yards down the road. I accepted and as we walked he told me in broken English how busy he was preparing for the event. With a pained look, he said he expected two hundred contestants this year. He was feeling a little overwhelmed.

"But it wasn't anywhere near that big last year," I said.

"Retrorunning is gaining very much now. It is international," he said, waving his hands at me. "You are here, no?"

I agreed that I was here and that the race was therefore international. But he said that he also expected competitors to come from all over Europe.

"What about Stefano Morselli?" I asked, suddenly flushing nervously at the thought of the world's best backward runner. But Paolo told me that Morselli had hurt himself training and probably wouldn't run. With Morselli out of the race, my chances of placing improved dramatically. To hide my glee, I asked Paolo what made Morselli so good.

"He really want the pig," Paolo said.

"What pig?"

"The Parma pig," he responded. He explained that the first year he organized the Golden Shrimp, in 1992, he took out an ad in the local paper and offered a giant leg of ham from the city of Parma as first prize. Morselli saw the ad, wanted the ham, trained hard, and won first place.

"It is very good ham," Paolo said, after I told him the right word for the meat. "He wanted it again, so he keep winning every year. He is winning all the first hams."

As Veerabadran said, everybody has to make their own meaning. For Morselli, it was all about great ham.

Poviglio turned out to be a pretty little town. It had a small cobblestoned square, with an old church on one side and three cafés on the other. It was surrounded by vineyards and fields of melon, and you could hear the church bell ring from just about anywhere in town. Since Paolo was so busy preparing for the race, I spent the next day with Camelia, his wife. When we weren't out in public, she quickly dropped her haughtiness and smiled. She was mostly bashful, but her wild black hair—which hung down to the small of her back—and her striking looks created an impression of rock star arrogance. It was fun to be around her—everyone in Poviglio, men and women, stopped what they were doing to watch her walk past.

Camelia was Romanian and had met Paolo while he was on vacation in eastern Europe. She wasn't alone in Poviglio. It turned out that a lot of the good-looking women in town were Romanians who had married Poviglian men. I asked one of them how she had met her husband and she said that he, too, had gone on vacation to Romania. The husbands were mostly overweight, balding, or both, but the men invariably seemed extremely pleased with themselves.

While it was interesting to learn about the ties between Poviglio and Romania, I was getting antsy. I couldn't wait for the race to start. I hadn't come all this way to chat with good-looking Romanian women. I wanted to run, and it was a form of torture to spend the day doing nothing. I've always felt that I can do anything as long as I don't have to wait too long and think about it. But when I do have to wait, I tear myself apart minute by minute until I have no strength left. At least the race was early Saturday morning. I wouldn't have to waste another day.

To better prepare, I told Camelia that I would meet her and Paolo for dinner and went back to the hotel so I could walk the racecourse. When Gianpietro had dropped me off, he had pointed down the road and said that the course went to a small roadside market and then doubled back. I set out to build a mental map of the ground I had to cover. The race began at a tall statue of two winged angels that stood a block away from the town square. The first quarter mile was a pretty, tree-lined straightaway that would also be the home stretch when we doubled back. After the straightaway there was a sharp left turn onto the country highway that ran in front of my hotel. The bulk of the race was on this road. On one side there were fields of wheat and corn interspersed between one-story factories. The other side was dotted with small country houses.

As I walked, I periodically turned around so I could see what the road looked like backward. I tried to memorize the stages of the race—the first cornfield, the tile factory—so that I could pace myself as I ran.

I got to the roadside market and went inside to double-check that it was the correct turnaround. The guy behind the counter spoke decent English and walked outside with me to show me how it would be organized. Last year, he said, the race had started here. He had watched it and was amused. He said he was one of the few to see it.

As we talked, I heard the approach of a blaring PA system. Suddenly, a small Fiat drove past at 40 mph followed by a long line of honking cars that wanted to go faster. Two loudspeakers were strapped to the roof of the Fiat and Paolo sat in the passenger seat, announcing the Golden Shrimp in a rapid monotone. His driver was flustered by the traffic and had accelerated significantly beyond the optimal advertising speed.

"Venite a vedere il Gambero d'Oro questo sabato!" he yelled as fast as he could to compensate. Come watch the Golden Shrimp this Saturday!

By the time I processed what was going on, they had already disappeared around a bend.

"You see?" said the storekeeper with a shrug. "Nobody in Poviglio can understand what is happening. It is madness. But you must be mad to run backward, no?"

At dinner that night at Paolo's house, I asked why he called the race the Golden Shrimp. He opened and closed his hand through the air like Pac-Man moving backward. Shrimp, he said, are one of the few animals that move backward. It was the first image that occurred to him ten years ago.

I asked if he ran backward when he was growing up in Poviglio and he told me that this was not his hometown. He said he was born and raised in a town half a mile down the road. He didn't start retrorunning until he moved the half mile to Poviglio.

Nothing was making sense to me, so I decided to call it an early night and get a lot of sleep before the race. I asked Paolo if people started gathering at five in the morning or if five-thirty was good enough.

"Morning?" he said, perplexed. "The race is in the evening."

"I thought it was at six in the morning."

"No, no. It is at six in the evening."

Granted, there had been a language barrier between Gianpietro and me when I arrived. But the guy had obviously not tried very hard to be helpful and had confused me for no purpose. I could only hope that there wouldn't be any more confusion.

"You will win, you will win," Veerabadran squawked over the telephone. I had called him for some support from the pay phone in the hotel lobby. "Challenges are always, always. No challenge, no fun. Headstanding! Don't forget."

When we hung up, I went upstairs and stood on my head but couldn't last more than twenty seconds. All the Italian pizza I'd been eating weighed heavily on the roof of my stomach. It probably wasn't the type of power fuel I needed right now. I went back downstairs and called Tara. She soothed me with talk about her summer job and told me it was a good thing I was running so much because I was working off all the weight I had gained sumo-ing. When I hung up, I felt better.

Around three the next afternoon, wiry people began to appear in the hotel hallways. I asked one of them if he was here for the retrorunning and he said yes. I was thrilled. He was twenty years old and had a monstrously large nose, kind eyes, and a lisp. His name was Riccardo and together we went downstairs, where he introduced me to his mother, father, and various members of his running club. They were from Pisa and over the past few years had become enthusiastic backward runners.

Riccardo particularly liked retrorunning because he had severe asthma and found that he couldn't run more than two miles forward or backward. Running such a short distance forward wasn't much of a challenge, but doing it backward was very demanding. His father, a scraggly-bearded man in his late fifties, was an extreme runner. He did sixty-mile runs—something his son could never hope to achieve. But retrorunning gave them a chance to run together, and for that reason the family had embraced it wholeheartedly.

Riccardo told me that they even put on their own retrorunning race in Pisa. Last year, they had twenty people. This year, there were sixty. He felt like there was a surge in interest in the sport. Events were popping up every weekend around Europe. "Many people run forward in Italy," he said, "but now many people are switching."

I followed Riccardo and his family to the town square and was surprised to see well over a hundred men and women in serious running garb. Many had matching outfits and pristine new shoes. They wore super-short shorts with slits to allow for maximum leg movement. One woman wore a track bikini, like the kind sprinters wear in the Olympics. It showed off her powerful legs and rippled stomach.

I was wearing a pair of lightweight running shorts (not the super-short variety) and the tank top I had run my marathon in. Since the tank top was a few years old, it felt way out of fashion, particularly here in Italy. The other competitors glanced at me and looked away dismissively. I hurriedly made my way to the registration desk, which was set up in the town square.

On the way, I overheard a young guy speaking English with an American accent. "An American!" I shouted impulsively, though I rudely interrupted the conversation he was having with a German runner.

"You're American, too?" he said, equally astonished. He was tall and had the good-natured optimism of a guy from the Midwest. "Wow, this is really great."

His name was Brian Godsey and he had just graduated from college in Ohio. He was in Italy in part to study Italian for the summer, but he admitted now, to the German and to me, that the real reason he came was to run the Golden Shrimp. The summer language course was just a cover to convince his parents to let him go. He was a serious runner—he had been an NCAA star in college and had run at the nationals in the five thousand meters. But he felt that he had taken forward running as far as he could, and about six months ago he began running backward. Now the sport dominated his life.

I liked him immediately. Being here with other retrorunning en-
thusiasts was such an overwhelmingly happy experience for him, I
thought he might cry. As we talked, I realized that he knew far more
about the sport than I did. He knew about Veerabadran ("He's totally
amazing, I can't believe you met him. Is he cool?"), and had also
memorized the times of other runners from around the world. He
asked me if I knew about Thomas Dold of Germany or Stefania
Zambello of Italy.

We went to the registration desk together and I noticed that many
had signed up as part of a team. After consulting Brian, we wrote in
our names together followed by "Team RetroUSA. Membership: 2."
The lady behind the desk handed us our numbers and a specially
manufactured padded helmet with the words "oɪteRЯunning" emblazoned on the side.

It proved Tara right—retrorunners did wear helmets. This one
strapped around my head like a sweatband with extra thickness in
the back. It was meant to protect only the back of the head in the
event of a fall, but the padding was too thin to be of much use. Plus,
the helmet made me look ridiculous. I noticed that Brian and I were
two of only a few to wear them. But I knew that Tara would want me
to wear it, so I kept it on.

Brian went to talk with an Italian runner and Paolo quickly trotted up to me. "This is Brian Godsey," he said, wide-eyed and near ecstasy. "He is here, with us. I cannot believe it."

Paolo told me that Brian had made headlines in the retrorunning
community three months ago when he ran the backward mile in
6:10 minutes, a new world record. Brian, it turned out, was one of
backward running's hottest young stars.

I didn't believe Paolo. Brian was a nice guy, but he didn't look half
as intimidating as the German runners, who had shaved heads, pink
running shoes, and green tank tops. The muscles on their calves
bulged and they scowled at everyone. They threw their padded helmets away and scoffed at those of us who wore them. Brian and I
were fashion misfits. He actually looked worse than I did. He was

wearing an old T-shirt and normal, lightweight swim trunks. It was like he was just popping out of the dorm for a quick jog, though the padded helmet might have suggested he was spastic or epileptic.

A sagging sign hung between two buildings, demarcating the start line. It read SPORT E FÈSTA—Sport Is a Party. A white line was painted beneath it, and the runners began to line up. It was now 5:50 P.M. Ten minutes until race time. Paolo was right—there were about 150 runners gathered.

Lining up was odd. Everyone found a position and then turned around. It didn't feel right, particularly when they took the official race photo. I had to crane my neck around in order to respond to the "Formàggio!" command. A lot of people just smiled without turning their heads, so anyone who sees the picture will just have to assume that the crowd was smiling.

Brian and I stuck together and took a position toward the left side of the line. I had forgotten about the jostling for position that occurs at footraces. Runners who got to the line a little late had to start from the wings or try pushing their way in. Brian held his arms away from his body and stiffened them to preserve his space, and I copied the technique. The race line was three rough rows of people shoulder-to-shoulder across the whole street and everyone was hopping from foot to foot and taking deep breaths.

My heart was racing. With all the competitions I'd been in, you'd think I would have gotten used to it by now, but I never did. I was frantic and felt a mounting sickness. It all came down to this start line, these Germans, my training, Veerabadran's wisdom, and the street behind me. I thought of Tara and imagined her watching me now. It made me feel stronger.

The Fiat with the megaphone pulled up—this was the pace car that would drive ahead of the runners. An older man in a sweater vest stood at the edge of the start line and readied the start gun. I remembered running on the beach with Veerabadran. The road beneath my feet was clean and solid. My heart rate slowed down.

Pop! The gun made my shoulders jerk up convulsively but I took off backward, tightly packed among the other runners. It was dangerous and I was glad that I was wearing my helmet, if only for psychological reasons. There were too many people hauling ass backward. I realized that I could be responsible for getting out of the way of only the people I could see. If someone was moving faster than me, they couldn't see that they were moving up on me, but since I was watching them approach, it was best for me to move aside. Likewise, I immediately gave up on looking over my shoulder and assumed that the people behind me would move if I overtook them. Otherwise they would get trampled.

Brian sprinted away at the start and disappeared. Within one hundred yards, I fell into a compact group of a few runners who were all moving at the same pace. A guy in his early thirties led me by about eight feet, and then there was an older man following me ten feet away. As I came to the end of the tree-lined straightaway, it seemed like there were only about twenty people running slower than me. But I felt like I was running at the top end of what my endurance could sustain. I was definitely moving faster than I had trained for, but I felt okay and told myself just not to move any faster.

It was hard not to speed up. I naturally wanted to overtake the guy leading me and it wouldn't have taken much in the short term. But I knew that if I were to move even a little faster, I would quickly run out of energy, so I stayed in the formation. The others must have felt the same way, as none of us tried to pass.

We settled into a rhythm of pain and then sank further into despair. I hit the wall at five minutes and entered the wildfire-in-my-calves zone. But Veerabadran had trained me well. I was prepared for the pain. It didn't hurt any less, but I was able to check out of my body and put it on cruise control. I thought about Tara. I brought her image into my mind and repeated her name like a mantra. I closed my eyes.

"Kick ass, Josh!"

I was shocked out of my trance by the sight of Brian racing backward toward the finish line on the other side of the road. The shoddy race car led him by a few feet. I didn't understand what was happening at first. Had something gone wrong? Did Brian get lost? And then I realized that he had already made it to the halfway point and had now doubled back, heading for the end. Brian was moving so fast, it was difficult to comprehend. The driver of the Fiat was frantically trying to stay ahead of him but couldn't get much acceleration in second gear. Brian wasn't looking over his shoulder so he didn't know that he was in danger of smashing into the start car. He had moved beyond pain; his legs were moving so fast, it looked like he was floating above the pavement. There was no one anywhere near him on the other side of the road.

"Holy shit, Brian!" I yelled back as we hurtled away from each other on opposite sides of the road. I could hear him laugh as he sped past, effortlessly threatening the Fiat and headed for the record books. According to my watch, he was going to beat Morselli's record by at least a full minute. I felt like a crewman on a ship sailing into uncharted waters. No one had ever run backward like he was running right now. It was revolutionary for the sport. He wasn't just running faster than anyone before him—he was establishing a new retrorunning frontier.

It boosted me through my suffering. I knew that the halfway point was far away, but thinking about Brian's achievement was a good distraction. Still, by the time I reached the turnaround, my legs felt like they were going to give out and I began to lose hope. So far, my heels hadn't been catching on the ground, the telltale sign of imminent collapse. But as I rounded the turnaround cone, the unfamiliar turning motion shocked my legs. They buckled, my right heel caught, and I almost fell. Recovering from the stumble cost me precious energy and revealed my legs to be weaker than I had thought. It was a sickening thing to discover with almost a mile left to go.

The thirty-year-old guy in front of me must have been in worse shape because suddenly he appeared on my side and slowly dropped back. He stanched the loss ten feet past me and then began to recover. I didn't want him to retake me so I matched his renewed attack pace, but it cost me everything I had. I had now used up my reserves and was running on fumes.

It worked. I kept him about five feet away as we rounded the curve back onto the tree-lined home stretch. I heard a crowd of people shouting my name and saw my hotel's staff lining the road. Salvatore pumped his fist in the air and shouted, *"Andiamo, Joshua!!"*

The finish line was three hundred yards away. It might as well have been three hundred miles. It was too much. I had nothing left. I could feel myself inadvertently slowing down and the runners trailing me began to move up. I started cursing myself until I heard a strange bouncing sound behind me. I didn't have the strength to turn around—all my energy was funneled into staying upright. But I didn't need to turn around to know that it was Tara running behind me. I even understood that she had deliberately not worn a bra so that the sound of her bouncing tits would inspire and motivate me in my darkest moment.

She wasn't alone. I could sense a lot more behind my back now. There was a nice house on a hill in San Francisco. It was yellow with blue trim. Two babies slept by the window in a powder-blue room. In the backyard, a little black puppy frolicked with a five-hundred-pound Parma pig. The sky was vivid blue and the sun strong.

The distance between me and my pursuers stopped shrinking and then I began to expand my lead. The old man trailing me suddenly caught a heel and went down hard on his coccyx. The paramedics at the finish line rushed toward him, passing me as I rocketed toward the end. I wasn't even aware that I was running anymore. The future floated behind me and warmed my back. I had never run so fast— forward or backward. I was propelled by an all-encompassing bliss. All my questions were being answered.

The finish line flowed out from under my feet. It seemed like the pavement was a river and I was simply watching the water flood past. But then the water spiked toward me, as if dam operators had opened the floodgates. A race aide caught me before I hit the ground. He held me up, but when I tried to turn around to walk forward, I collapsed again. My legs had nothing left. The aide slung my arm over his shoulder, dragged me to the low wall surrounding the winged-angel statue, and returned to the finish line to catch others. Almost everybody fell at the end.

I didn't win. As far as I could tell, I didn't even get close. But I had won something else, something much more valuable than ham. I knew what I wanted the future to look like. I couldn't control the unknowns, but that didn't mean I wasn't going to run as fast into it as I could. In fact, I realized that this was the key to my happiness.

Brian found me slumped underneath the angels. I managed to stand up long enough to shake his hand. I didn't know my time yet, but many knew that Brian had finished first and broken the record

Stefano Morselli

by more than a minute. I was very proud to be on Team RetroUSA. People looked at him with awe. Paolo came over, pumped his hand, and kept saying, "Incredible." Brian gave an aw-shucks shrug. As more and more people found out what he had done, they came over to congratulate him. He scratched the back of his head, shifted from foot to foot, and smiled a big goofy smile.

The awards ceremony in the town square was a celebration of Brian's achievement, but Paolo started by calling me to the stage. I had posted a 16:24 time, which placed me twentieth in the men's division, the last position to receive a prize. When I clambered onstage, Paolo handed me a small rounded ball of vacuum-packed bologna. He told the crowd that I had won three quarters of a kilogram of meat.

Brian did substantially better. He won an all-expenses-paid trip to Sardinia (all expenses paid from Poviglio, that is, so he'd have to come back to get to Sardinia). Second prize was a large pig's leg with the hoof still on it. Brian was doubly glad to have placed first; he wouldn't have wanted to backpack around Italy with a pig's leg. The mayor of Poviglio shook his hand and draped an Italian flag around his neck. He also gave him a large hunk of hard cheese. The mayor gave me a picture book depicting the refugee crisis in Eritrea. I have no idea why.

Still, I was pleased. I had done much better than expected and had even won prizes. When I phoned Tara, she was duly impressed with the bologna and the book. I told her that I was bringing them home to her as a sign of my love. She said she couldn't wait.

Riku Jaro

CHAPTER FIVE

A FAMILY THAT BATHES
TOGETHER, STAYS TOGETHER

Despite being very close, my mom and I were having trouble getting along. It was the type of closeness that's characterized by a lot of fuming and tense conversation. We disagreed about almost everything but still talked on the phone every other night. We argued about why I didn't want to talk about Christmas in July, what she thought about my career, and why I wouldn't take sides when she got into arguments with her brothers and sisters. Over the years, we had slipped into a pattern of antagonism that had somehow become accepted. It wasn't good and I wanted to figure out a way to break out of it before I started my own family. It seemed important to me to get along with my own parents before becoming a parent myself. That's why I felt it was a good thing we went to central Finland for the Sauna World Championship. Because sometimes it takes a 220-degree sauna to clear the mind.

. . .

When I was thirteen, my mom and John decided to move us out of San Francisco. We were renting a small house on the edge of Golden Gate Park and the fog was overwhelming. Everybody was depressed, particularly John. He had borrowed a lot of money to build his city in the Kuwaiti desert. He thought they had a housing shortage but the price of oil fell, the houses never got built, and he had to declare bankruptcy. Mom told me that we needed to move to suburbia so that we could buy a house and build a sauna. John was Finnish, she explained, and every Finn needed a sauna. Without it, they were adrift in the world.

It seemed more likely to me that John was adrift in the world because he had just blown a dump-truck load of cash, but I wasn't going to mention it. I was happy to get out of the fog. That is, I was happy until I saw the house. It was twenty-five miles north of the city in farm country. There were lots of cows and rolling, sunburned golden hills. I hated it. We were moving from a big city to nowheresville. Plus, the house was part of a new subdivision—the place looked like every other house on the street.

It threatened the way I had been raised to think of myself. My mother always told me that we were descended from greatness. As proof, she said we were direct descendants of John Adams and taught me the concept of noblesse oblige when I was six. Even right after my parents' divorce, when my mom didn't have enough money to pay our electric bill, she explained by candlelight that I was going to do great things. I did not belong in suburbia.

But, at the time, the family had more important things to deal with than my injured pride. In addition to the bankruptcy, John was fighting a custody battle with his ex-wife. Erik, my stepbrother, was six months older than me and already boasted about twice my weight. I was unusually skinny, but Erik was uncommonly fat. He ate candy all the time, probably as a reaction to the stress of the divorce.

When we first met at age ten, Erik and I didn't get along. I'd call him fat, and he'd sit on me. I was so skinny, I couldn't get away. I quickly stopped calling him names, but I felt vindicated when he got shipped off to a fat farm when we were twelve. He came back depressed and ate nothing but dry popcorn and jicama.

The custody battle got worse when John's ex-wife became a born-again Christian. She found Jesus and Jesus told her that John was a major international drug kingpin who was in league with the Devil. I kind of wished he was a narco-trafficker. It would have been more exciting than life in suburbia. Either way, Erik believed her (at least about the Satan part) and moved to her apartment. Alissa, my nine-year-old stepsister, stayed with us.

So when we moved to the suburban house on Highland Street, the family was in disarray. Erik spent the weekends with us but it was difficult for him to speak with John, who he feared might be Satan's high priest. It only got worse when John insisted that we spend the summer building a sauna together. He thought it would help us bond as a family, but it only convinced Erik that John really was Satan and needed a hell pit to roast in.

Still, we were stuck in suburbia for the summer with nothing to do. None of us had any friends, since we were new to town, and we were too far from the city to easily see our old friends. John handed me a pickax, gave Erik a shovel, and told us to get to work.

The house was on a slope. To create room for the sauna, we needed to bust through one of the cookie-cutter walls in the cookie-cutter house and excavate the hillside under the building. It was one of John's typically ambitious plans—never did he consider the possibility that it was beyond the powers of two thirteen-year-old boys who didn't like each other or their lives.

That summer, we dug. And eventually we talked. Our voices had changed. Erik had also found Jesus. I had found Buddha. I thought Erik was a dangerous extremist. He thought I was a dangerous extremist. We started to get along.

The sauna took shape. I remember the first time I smelled the cedar planking. When we laid it down in the hole we had dug, it seemed like the forest had sprouted in what was once a dark, spider-filled underground crawl space. John began speaking the Finnish his mother had taught him and instructed us on the proper pronunciation of sauna: *sow*(as in a pig)-*nuh*. When he dropped an armful of cedar on his foot, he said, "Satan, get thee behind me," in his family's Finnish dialect. Erik ran to get the ice. It was the first time he had been nice to his dad in months.

Two months later, the sauna stove arrived on the back of a truck. After hooking it up, John sat the whole family down in the living room and went over the sauna rules. First, there would be no farting in the sauna. Erik, Alissa, and I started giggling. John silenced us with an icy look and asked Erik if he would fart in church.

"No," Erik said.

"Then don't fart in the sauna either," John said. "It's like a church. But it's also good for your skin."

The other rules were more mundane: Open the vent if you're the last one out, put a towel between your butt and the wood, and don't get water on the wood. We had been in his mother's sauna in Oregon but this was different. This was our sauna now and we were old enough to learn how to take care of it.

That night, we turned the stove on for the first time, and, according to Finnish tradition, the three men went in first. It was a strange, solemn experience. We stripped naked. Erik and I tried to wrap a towel around ourselves as fast as we could without looking like we cared. John just dropped his trousers, flung open the door, shouted something urgent in Finnish, and leaped in, slamming the door behind him.

Erik and I cautiously opened the door. A blast of heat hit us in the face.

"For God's sake, get in here and shut the door before you let all the heat out," John shouted.

We stepped inside and sat on the top bench. I got wedged in between Erik and John. The sauna wasn't very big—the three of us had to sit shoulder-to-shoulder, which was a little uncomfortable at 160 degrees. John threw a ladleful of water on the rocks and a powerful burst of steam smacked us in the face.

"Ahh!" Erik and I gasped.

"Doesn't that feel good?" John asked, and he threw another one on. He looked at me and smiled.

"How many houses do you know have a sauna?" he asked. "We may look like all the others on the outside, but inside, we're a little different."

A few months later, Erik moved back in with us, and John hung a sign above the sauna door. It said A FAMILY THAT BATHES TOGETHER, STAYS TOGETHER.

This past March, I flew up to Portland, Oregon, to visit the family. Erik picked me up at the airport. We were both twenty-nine now and Erik was a Lutheran minister in the Portland area. He no longer believed we were days away from the apocalypse or that Buddha was Satan. His religious views had mellowed over the years. He'd settled into a worldly theology that mixed God, video games, girls, Jesus, stereo equipment, and beer.

We stayed up all night drinking and playing violent video games with the volume up really loud. He was particularly proud of his subwoofer, which drove the neighbors in his apartment building crazy. If the police showed up, they'd find a whiskey-soaked kid preacher clutching a Bible and a joystick. He thought it would be easier to talk them out of citing him with his collar on.

Despite the late-night antics, he was a great pastor. He visited all the sick old people in the hospital and cried when they died. He gave impassioned sermons, stayed late at the church almost every night, and had an excellent singing voice. He was good-looking in a hefty sort of way (fat camp had done the trick but no one would accuse him of being skinny) but he hadn't been on a date in years.

The problem was that his social life was tied up with the church and he was prohibited from dating or even really flirting with anyone in the congregation. If he did and something went wrong, he could lose his job. But since he spent all his time at the church, he never met anyone else. "I never thought seminary would be the romantic high point of my life," he complained.

He said that he started online dating but got a lot of deviants looking for priests. The first few times he tried explaining that he wasn't a priest—he was a pastor—but he eventually just removed the job title from his bio. He put "Social Services" instead.

"I'm just a normal guy with a libido," he said on the two-hour drive out to the coast the day after I arrived. "I don't want to talk about God right off the bat with a woman. I want to talk about other things."

By the time we got to our parents' house, Erik had talked himself into a funk. He was sure that he'd never meet the right woman and get married. I wasn't feeling much better. Just the thought of spending a weekend with my mom was oppressive. In person, I couldn't just hang up the phone and end my trauma.

"Fil-ill-lil-loo!" she shouted when she saw us driving down the narrow road toward the house. It was an old family greeting that had supposedly been handed down over the generations, maybe all the way from John Adams. But I couldn't imagine the president of the United States standing by the side of the road and crowing like a rooster.

The old filililoo shout never failed to embarrass me. As a child, when I strayed a bit too far from her in a crowded place, she would start shouting it at the top of her lungs and wouldn't stop until I came running back. It was a striking sight because my mom is particularly beautiful. Even now, wearing a forest-green sweat suit on this drizzly Oregon day in an isolated community of fishermen and loggers, she maintained the aura of the fashion model and beauty queen she once was. She stood with one foot in front of the other, perfectly poised, and yodeled again, this time showing her sparkling white teeth.

I gave her a hug and she asked me if I remembered filililoo.

"Of course I do," I said. "How could I forget? It's really embarrassing."

"Well, you're twenty-nine now," she said, pinching my cheek. "You're too old to be embarrassed by your mother."

She was right. And yet, I was embarrassed. It wasn't something I really understood. Before we became a stepfamily, I had been an only child. But even after she gained two more children through the marriage, her love for me was still overbearing and suffocating. It felt particularly so now when she immediately launched into a discussion of when I was going to visit next.

"Can't we enjoy each other's company for two seconds before you start stressing about when we're going to see each other again?" I asked.

I had repeatedly told her we would get along a lot better if she didn't press me to commit to visiting. Nor did I want to go over the details of what we were going to eat on any given holiday. I wasn't interested. It wouldn't be a good conversation. It never was.

"I was just thinking we could come to San Francisco for a visit next month," she started off. "What's a good weekend for you and Tara?"

Moving back to his hometown had been good for John, but it hadn't been good for my mom. She had lived in Vegas, New York, Milan, Los Angeles, and San Francisco. She had spent her life in or near big cities. In Seaside, at the northwestern tip of Oregon, there was no outlet for her. There was no opera house, museum of art, or transcendental meditation center. She was one of the few vegetarians in the area and had to bring her own tofu with her when she went out to the local restaurants. She spent her time thinking about going on meditation retreats in California and seeing me.

It was a vicious cycle. The more she obsessed about seeing me, the less I wanted to see her. She could sense my anger and sat down at the dining room table to mope.

"We haven't even talked about the cruise yet," she pouted.

"What cruise?" I snapped.

"There's this really great cruise in Australia," she said, brightening.

I groaned. Last year, she convinced all of us to take a cruise to Mexico. It turned out that it went from San Pedro Harbor in Los Angeles—one of the world's ugliest bulk-freight harbors—to Ensenada, Mexico, about 150 miles south. Inexplicably, it lasted four days. The captain drove us in zigzags around the Pacific in a mammoth, aging tub inappropriately named *The Ecstasy*. We ran out of the booze we brought the first night and were forced to pay eight dollars per pink plastic cup of weak, artificially flavored piña colada. It took fifty bucks per person to get tolerably drunk.

"That cruise was a low point in my life," I told her.

"It was fun."

"It was not fun."

"We got to see the blowhole."

She had me there. A few years before the cruise, on our last family vacation, we went to the Hawaiian island of Kauai and Mom took us to see the famous Spouting Horn. According to her guidebook, it was one of only three natural wave-driven geysers in the world. When an incoming wave slammed into the cliff, water was supposed to be forced through a crack in the rock and shoot up fifty feet into the air. When we got there, it was having trouble producing a two-foot-tall dribble. I could have pissed higher.

The second blowhole in the world was located outside of Ensenada. The cruise guides said it was the most interesting sight in the area, so we rented a cab and headed out. We were on a roll. Seeing two out of three blowholes in the world was about as much of an accomplishment as I could hope for from the cruise.

La Bufadora, as the blowhole was known, was an inlet in the barren coastline. To get there, we walked through a gauntlet of vendors hawking conch shells, cheap metal bracelets, and T-shirts printed with pictures of a giant, blazing geyser. But when we arrived at the seawall, we saw nothing. Water lolled around lazily in the inlet. We asked the vendors where the geyser was, and they pointed to the T-shirts.

"You remember where the third blowhole is?" Mom asked me.

The third and final blowhole in the world was located somewhere in Australia.

"We could round out the collection," she said. "Imagine seeing all three blowholes in the world? It would be like climbing all the tall mountains in the world."

"It would be nothing like that, Mom. They're just blowholes. And they don't blow."

"They do blow," Erik said. "Just not literally."

"Another miserable blowhole is not going to entice me to get back on a boat with you," I said, ignoring Erik.

"You can bring more vodka," she offered.

"I don't think that's a healthy way of approaching the family vacation."

"Well, then, what do you want to do this summer?" she said, hurt that her long-savored plan had been so quickly rejected.

But here we were again. Scheduling. It was a recipe for a shouting match, and John could see me getting ready to say something mean.

"Sauna's fired up," he said cheerily. He was the family peacemaker. The more tense things got, the more laid-back he became.

The house's old sauna had seen better days. The wood was splotchily stained, and the cedar smell was underscored by a pronounced mustiness. But John had transplanted our little sign, hung it above the new family sauna, and we were still bathing together.

As usual, the boys started it off. Erik and I were accustomed now to the blast of the steam. We even liked it. Sometimes it got so hot, you had to breathe through your hands so you wouldn't scorch your lungs. But it still felt good. I thought of it as a force I couldn't fight. I had to surrender. My shoulders slumped, I resigned myself to the sting and relaxed.

After dumping a couple of ladles on the rocks, John said that he got an e-mail from Cousin Jinny in Finland today. She grew up in

Oregon with John but moved to Finland when she was in her thirties. According to Jinny, a small town in Finland had started up
a sauna competition a few years ago, and, since it was the only one,
it had become the Sauna World Championship. The organizers
were calling it a sport, and had even coined a name for it: extreme
sauna-ing. The concept was simple: whoever stays in the longest,
wins.

"Maybe that could be our summer vacation," John said. "There
aren't any blowholes in Finland, but there are large women who
come into the sauna and beat you with cedar branches. That's a
sight."

John shook his head, remembering his trip to Finland as a young
man. He said the cedar-branch beating was an old Finnish tradition.
I told Erik that it was a better way to meet women than Match.com
and he scowled at me.

I figured Mom was going to keep coming up with asinine vacation
ideas, so the rest of us might as well come up with one of our own.
Plus, John said that first prize was a new sauna, and the one we were
in now needed replacing.

"Will they ship it to the U.S.?" I asked.

"They won't have any choice if we win," he said.

"No," my mom said. "Absolutely not. We're going on a cruise to
someplace warm."

"It'll be plenty warm in the sauna," John said.

Mom glared at him until he said he was going to take Fred the dog
for a walk. Erik went with him, leaving me alone with her. She was
quiet for a moment.

"If we do this—and I'm just saying *if*," she said, "there's no way
I'm competing. It might cause wrinkles."

Wrinkles were the number-one enemy in her life and the battle
was pitched. She threw an impressive array of lotions and creams

into the fray and had so far succeeded admirably. But she wasn't about to take any risks and I knew better than to argue.

"I'll go if you promise to be nice to me," she said suddenly.

My throat stiffened and I felt my eyes tear up. It was all I wanted, to be nicer to her. I wanted us to be happy. I just wasn't sure we could actually pull it off. But the sauna had always brought the family together. Maybe it could help us all one more time.

Alissa was no longer the nine-year-old girl that my mom used to dress up in pink, frilly outfits. She was now a twenty-five-year-old militant lesbian with a shaved head, combat boots, and a construction job. She recently fell in love with a thirty-nine-year-old woman—our parents didn't know about that yet—and had become distanced from the family. For the past couple of years, she had skipped the holidays and family vacations, so it wouldn't be easy to convince her to come, particularly after the *Ecstasy* cruise. Erik was closest with her, but even he rarely saw her.

That was partially because she was easy to miss. She grew up in the shadow of two talkative brothers and had developed a quiet, disappearing personality. When my mom broke out the photo albums to reminisce about past family vacations, somebody would inevitably point to Alissa and say, "I didn't remember you being on that trip."

She wouldn't say anything in response. But in her eyes, you could see it hurt her. She felt that Erik, John, my mom, and I made up the nucleus of the family and that she was treated as an afterthought. Erik and I were the same age and went through school together. We always had something to talk about and Alissa couldn't participate in that. But now we were all adults, had been out of school for years, and I was fascinated to know who she had become.

Erik and I called her that night from the beach and invited her on the trip. We told her that we couldn't compete as a family without her. Plus, she had been working outside all summer and had the thickest skin of all of us. Erik mentioned the big women with the cedar branches, but she said she already had a girlfriend. She pointed out that Erik had more romantic frustrations than she did.

"We all really want you to come along," I said and handed the phone to John.

"It's your heritage, missy," he said. "We're going back to the homeland."

"There's lots of nice lesbians in Helsinki," Mom shouted over his shoulder.

I grabbed the phone back. "She means it's very gay-friendly," I said. "Listen, it won't be the same without you. If you don't come, we won't have anyone to ignore."

"What?" she said.

"I'm just kidding. Seriously, though, it won't be the same without you."

The other end of the line was quiet.

"When are we going?" she finally asked.

The Sauna World Championship billed itself as "the hottest event of the summer." It took place in early August in the small southern Finnish town of Heinola, though would-be contestants had to submit the entry form and a doctor's letter months in advance. The doctor's letter was required because the competition sauna was hot enough to kill you. Organizers pointed out that they kept the temperature at 212 degrees Fahrenheit, the temperature at which water boils. No American doctor in his right mind would have authorized even the healthiest person to essentially cook himself, so we needed to find another way of getting the letter.

John said he had a doctor friend who might help us and promised to visit him later in the day. He came back that afternoon with letters for all of us. They were from Dr. Ed Point (R.P.) at the Point Medical Clinic in Astoria and confirmed that each of us was in good health and able to "physically compete in a Sauna Contest." I was impressed with John's connections—we didn't even have to see the guy—until I read the Point Medical Clinic's staff list, which was printed on the left side of the letterhead. The R.P. after Ed Point's name signified that he was a board-certified "Renaissance Physician." The staff included a urologist named Peter Stickler, a dermatologist named Mark Wartly, and a gynecologist named Seymour Lipps.

"Johhhhn," my mom said with rising cadence. "A gynecologist named Seymour Lipps?"

"He's got great hands," John said with a boyish grin and then admitted that he had forged the letters. "But the Finns will never figure it out. They're a bunch of lunkheads."

We decided to fax in the letters along with our entry forms—the organizers could do no worse than deny us entry. But a few weeks later, we received a letter welcoming us as contestants. Maybe the Finns were used to crackpot doctors—their docs were, after all, certifying people to fry their brains.

As if anticipating the potential medical fallout, *The New York Times Magazine* ran an article the following weekend that described the plight of a thirty-five-year-old man who had taken a sauna. A few hours after the sauna, the guy lost his memory, started vomiting, became belligerent, and had to be rushed to the emergency room. The doctors determined that he had overhydrated himself after the sauna and diluted the sodium levels in his blood. It was a condition that can cause "seizures, coma and even death." It took him a week to recover. It wasn't drugs or a rare infection. He just drank too much water. I didn't even know you could drink too much water. This was how the sauna could mess you up. It turned normal bodily functions like sweating, breathing, and drinking into potentially life-threatening activities.

This family vacation was going to be unlike any other. Not only would we have to survive a week in close proximity to one another, we had to contend with what most people would call a steam cooker. We needed, as a family, to take our sauna skills to the next level. So, in May, I flew back up to Oregon to do some research. There were dangerous holes in our understanding. For instance, according to the contest welcome letter, the name of the event was not the World Sauna Championship. That was the subtitle beneath the official name, which was the "Löyly MM." We had no idea what that meant.

To figure it out, Erik and I drove to Finnware, a Finnish goods shop in Astoria, about twenty minutes up the road from Seaside. I picked up a copy of *Saunas: A Collection of Works, Mostly in English, by Finnish-Canadians, Finnish-Americans, and Finns.* It was a simple white paperback that contained a mixture of essays, short stories, and poems on the sauna, and, in keeping with the forthright presentation, the publishers had leveled with the reader. The reviews on the back cover were not flattering. "Some of these stories are better than the others," commented someone named Cold Omaha. "Could be better," opined a sheet-metal worker named Rick Tuura.

But after I flipped past a couple of poems ("Oh Sauna, My Sauna," "Fashioned for Heat"), I stumbled across an angry but enlightening screed. It was titled "Advancing the Sauna Principle," and it told me that the essential principle of the sauna—its very essence—was *löyly*. Bingo!

Unfortunately, Giles Ekola, the author, immediately informed his readers that *löyly* could not be translated into any language. More specifically, he said it could not, must not, and absolutely should never be translated as "steam." *Löyly*, he specified, is what happens to water when it is poured over hot sauna rocks. Calling the moist warmth that billows up off the rocks steam is "an error of the insufficient gathering of facts."

Under a big, bold subheading, Ekola clarified that "*Löyly* and Steam Are Different," and then supplied this definition: "*Löyly* should be translated as vaporized moisture that is in a process of drying." That sounded a lot like steam to me. Ekola must have realized that he was not convincing anyone, so he tried to browbeat the reader with a nearly hysterical, rapid-fire attack: "*Löyly* is the essential principle of the sauna; steam is not. *Löyly* is the objective of the sauna design, materials, and constructions; steam is not. *Löyly* gently draws perspiration from the body; steam does not. . . . For the sauna, *löyly* satisfies; steam does not."

He softened a bit, though, when he helped the reader pronounce *löyly*, which was about the only thing I found useful. He coached me to say "ler" and then "lew": ler-lew. This exercise "makes it possible for non-Finnish-speaking persons to lose their fear of the word, to accept it as a gentle friend and to pronounce and possess it as their own easily and readily." It sounded like he wanted to have sex with the word.

But at least I knew now that *löyly* meant steam and that I was never supposed to say that. It was like a code word for a secret society. If we got to Finland and they pointed to the LÖYLY MM sign, we would say, "Ler-lew, mmmmmmm," and hopefully they'd let us in.

At dinner that night, we went over the other Finnish words we knew. John's grandmother spoke to him in Finnish, but, for some reason, the only phrases he remembered were "There's a car coming," "Satan get thee behind me," "The sauna is ready," and "Smell my belly button." He warned us never to use that last phrase. "Smell my belly button" was, according to John, the single worst thing you could say to a Finnish person. It was the "F#*k you, you useless m*thaf*!king sh*tbag" of the Finnish language.

"Do Finns not wash their belly buttons?" I asked.

"I don't know. Just don't say it," John snapped. He could count on one hand the number of times he had heard his mother say it and each one was a painful memory. He told us about the time his father mentioned that he actually didn't like the pineapple upside-down cake she'd been cooking him for thirty years. She thought it was his favorite but, like Alissa, Grandpa Niemi was a quiet person. He didn't comment on it until he was fifty-eight. He finally couldn't take it anymore and said so. She turned red, told him (in Finnish) to smell her belly button, and kept on cooking it.

That night, we started heating up the sauna rocks at five in the evening. By ten, the temperature was 280 degrees. That was primarily because John installed the thermometer directly above the sauna stove; when we got in, it didn't feel half that hot. Rather than move the wall mount for the thermometer somewhere that made sense, John got an old bronze boiler thermometer. This made even less sense. He kept it loose on the window ledge above the oven. When we got in, he scoffed at the wall thermometer, grabbed the brass one, screamed because it was so damn hot, and promptly dropped it. He did this more frequently than we would have liked to admit.

"It's metal, Pa," Erik said for the umpteenth time. "Metal gets hot. It's one of its properties."

"Okay, okay, I hear you," John said absentmindedly as he searched for the thermometer under the bench. He picked it up with his towel and, with evident satisfaction, announced that the temperature was 180. Because he'd made such a simple task so difficult, it gave him a perverse pleasure to supply this otherwise ordinary piece of data.

A temperature of 180 degrees was not exactly competition-worthy, but we couldn't get it any hotter. Our only choice was to pour water on the rocks. That would turn into steam—I mean *löyly*—which would convert the sauna's dry heat into a wet heat. Water has a greater heat capacity than air, meaning that water can hold a lot more heat energy than air at the same temperature. It's the difference between sitting in a 150-degree sauna and a 150-degree Jacuzzi—the Jacuzzi would kill you.

Erik dumped ladle after ladle onto the rocks, and in a matter of seconds we could barely open our eyes or breathe. Erik groaned and tried to breathe through his hand, which, according to the rules they sent us, was illegal. During the competition, you were supposed to sit with your elbows on your knees and you couldn't cover or touch any part of your body with your hands. I gave Erik a poke—it was important that we accustom ourselves to the rules. He blew hot air on me, which stung painfully. It was the sauna equivalent of a titty twister.

As with backward running, the pain was something that we had to embrace. The difference was that we didn't need to do anything but sit there and endure—no movement was allowed. What we needed was Vicodin.

When I got out of the sauna, I called Eric Poolman, my old college roommate who was getting both a medical degree and an MBA at Yale. He was one of the smartest people I knew.

"Under no circumstances will I prescribe you Vicodin," he said. "Absolutely not."

There went that plan.

"And while we're on the phone," he continued, "I advise you not to do this. It's totally nuts. And if you do go forward with it, don't take anything, not even an Advil or aspirin. You'll thin your blood and just cause yourself more problems." He sounded genuinely upset. "The best you can do is train to be lucky," he said. "Some people are just born with fewer pain receptors."

When I asked him how to train to be lucky, he instructed me to take a coin and concentrate on flipping only heads. I asked him if he had any real advice, and after a pause he recommended drinking a lot of water and eating salt in the days preceding the event. That would increase the amount of water I retained and allow me to sweat for longer when I was in the sauna.

Luckily, John had recently decided to get into the salt business. The two-hundredth anniversary of the Lewis and Clark expedition was approaching and, back in the day, the explorers had set up a salt evaporator just up the beach from us. According to John, the town of Seaside was famous for this saltworks. He thought that the world either knew or would soon discover that Lewis and Clark were in desperate need of salt when they arrived at the Pacific. As publicity for the anniversary grew, John believed there would be an insatiable craving for all things Lewis and Clark. In his mind, nothing could satisfy that appetite better than his cans of Lewis and Clark Sea Salt.

He'd already come up with cute four-ounce tin cans emblazoned with a silhouette of Lewis and Clark. And, when he discovered that www.lewisandclarkseasalt.com was actually still available, he pounced on it and commissioned an attractive website. The back of each tin told the history of the Lewis and Clark expedition from a salt aficionado's point of view (the expedition obtained four bushels of salt in Seaside and "were thus able to survive the trek back to civilization"—that is, it was the salt that got them back, not Sacagawea).

The past few times I'd gone to Oregon, we had obligatory family salt-packing time. Everybody sat around the dining room table and filled tins with salt from a burlap bag. The first time we did it, I realized that there was something wrong. The burlap sack indicated that the salt was from China, not Oregon. I asked John about it.

"The cans say 'Pure Pacific Ocean Sea Salt,'" he said. "And China's on the Pacific."

John explained that the ocean currents were such that the water off the coast of Oregon came in a clear arc from China and Japan (that's how the sardines were supposed to get here). In short, John argued that the salt in the Chinese water would have eventually ended up in Oregon anyway. Plus, nobody in the area actually made salt.

Maybe consumers suspected the truth, because they weren't buying, leaving John with 178 pounds of Chinese salt. The average American consumes about 7 pounds of salt per year, which meant that he had a twelve-and-a-half-year supply in his garage. In light of the overstock, John had generously agreed to donate a pound of the stuff to the family's sauna-training efforts. Since John's last name was Niemi (pronounced "Knee-me"), we decided to call ourselves the "Steamy Niemis" in honor of his support. And, in return, Lewis and Clark Sea Salt Enterprises became the official sponsor of the Steamy Niemis.

I wanted to get us a team uniform, but the event guidelines

strictly delineated the maximum length and size of competition swimwear. The regulation inseam was so short as to basically mean Speedos—something we rejected categorically. I went to a local clothing store and found boxer briefs made out of a material that supposedly wicked sweat away from the skin. I bought one for everyone and wrote "Steamy Niemi" on each waistband with an indelible marker.

When we filled salt tins now, we talked about sauna strategy. While discussing the merits of short and long breaths, I presented a bold and devious idea to the family. We could fart. The smell would drive everyone else out of the sauna, making us the champions. It would be our secret weapon. We just had to eat a lot of beans the night before the contest and then let it rip. Of course, we'd never do such a thing under normal sauna circumstances—it was the first rule of sauna. But this was war and all was fair.

"Absolutely not," John said, disgusted. "Didn't I teach you anything? You do not become the first family of sauna by farting your way to the top."

Two years ago, my mom took me to a spa in Cannon Beach, another small town about ten miles south of Seaside. She had booked a massage for herself; I was just planning on walking around the town, but the receptionist mentioned that they had a Scots Hose practitioner, which sounded somewhat sinister to me. She assured me that it was a "lovely water treatment." I didn't have anything else to do so I agreed to give it a try.

An attractive blond lady led Mom inside, and a second later a dark-haired, tattooed woman appeared and asked if I was the one who wanted the Scots Hose. She sounded surprised to have a client and, possibly to prevent me from changing my mind, quickly led me down a hallway into a room marked WATER TREATMENTS.

In the center of the room, an elaborate eighteen-nozzle super-high-pressure shower was suspended over a stainless steel table.

Trisha, the tattooed lady, referred to it as a "Vichy Rain Shower" and said that it was used by the French to bring mental patients out of fits. It seemed equally possible, judging by the name, that the Nazi-collaborating Vichy government in France used it to torture resistance fighters.

The room was tiled and lined with waist-high steel railing. In one corner, a large fire hose was coiled on the wall. Trisha told me to leave my clothes on the plastic chair in the opposite corner—I could keep my underwear on. After I stripped, she told me to grab on to the steel railing, spread my legs, and face the wall. I was now mostly naked and she was fully dressed, gripping a fire hose. I was not in a power position.

The "treatment" was one of the most painful things I've ever put my skin through. The blast from the fire hose felt like it was slicing into my flesh. "Doesn't it feel good?" Trisha yelled over the deafening roar of the water. I had images of civil rights marchers in the sixties getting blasted with fire hoses and was suddenly confused. Should I continue to stand here and take the pain in solidarity with their experience? I realized that I was just a skinny white guy standing miserably in his wet underwear in a small Oregon town. This had nothing to do with civil rights.

But I now grasped that it had a lot to do with the sauna. Scots Hose was the perfect way to build the mental tools necessary for enduring a large amount of skin pain. While Trisha was attacking my backside with the high-pressure water, my analysis of the relationship between the civil rights movement and my predicament got me through the ten-minute treatment. There was actually something to be gained from the Hose.

A few weeks before the contest, Erik and I drove to Trisha's new spa in Astoria to see what more we could learn, though I hadn't told Erik much about the Hose. In fact, I'd told him almost nothing other than that we were going to get massages to "loosen up."

"Come on in and let me pressure-wash you," Trisha said enthusiastically when we arrived. She had taken over an old bank building and told us that the walls were so thick, nobody would hear a thing. Erik glanced at me warily and asked her what she meant. She explained the difference between Scots Hose and the Vichy Rain Shower but added that she could combine the treatments. Erik rolled his face into an ugly scowl and asked her to excuse us for a moment.

Trisha handed us each a pair of disposable underwear (clients didn't like getting their own underwear wet) and told us she'd be waiting down the hall.

"Are you crazy?" Erik demanded after Trisha disappeared through a door. I explained my pain theory and he shook his head in stubborn disbelief.

"Just put the goddamn undies on and get the fuck out there," I hissed, deciding to take the tough-love approach. "If you can't handle a five-foot-tall woman with a hose, how are you going to handle a 220-degree sauna?"

I'd always had a knack for convincing Erik to do things he didn't want to do. When we were kids, it usually involved jumping off buildings and diving under the garage door as it closed. But as we got older, I got bolder. A few years ago, I convinced him that he would meet the woman of his dreams on a Zimbabwean missionary expedition. The trip got canceled and Erik was heartbroken.

Ever since, Erik has been doubly wary of my ideas. Particularly now that he's a Lutheran pastor responsible for one of the most respected churches in Portland, it has become harder to convince him to do stupid things. But I reminded him that he'd already signed on for the family vacation and the family vacation would involve sitting in an extremely hot sauna. If he didn't train, it was going to be even more painful. He should think of Trisha as a sort of sauna coach.

He hastily grabbed the disposable undies from me, pulled them on, and stormed down the hallway. I heard Trisha greet him, and then a heavy, waterproof door thudded shut.

Fifteen minutes later, Erik reappeared in the changing room. He was naked and dripping wet. The disposable undies were in tatters in his clenched fist. The color was drained from his face but he told me that he'd be okay.

That night, as a result of the water-thrashing Trisha gave him, he came down with a flu. He thought he had strep throat. His throat was so sore, he could barely speak, and he felt feverish. We were due to fly to Finland in four days. This was a serious problem, so I asked my mom if she had an enema bag. I had recently read a magazine article about the health benefits of coffee enemas—they supposedly detoxified the body. Mom told me there was an enema bag under the sink, and while I was fishing it out she asked why I needed it.

"We're going to get aggressive and attack Erik's problem from both ends," I said. "We'll get him some throat lozenges and then we'll flush out all the toxins. We can't afford to let this progress."

"You're not getting near me with that thing," Erik whispered painfully when I held up the pink enema bag. I'd actually never given an enema. I asked my mom if they could be self-administered and she said they could.

"Good, because I don't know if I want to be involved in this," I said.

"I don't think *I* want to be involved in this," Erik rasped.

"Do you have any coffee beans?" I asked my mom. "Or maybe we should do a cold one. We could do an ice-cube enema. That'd stop the strep from dropping any lower."

"Yeah, because I'd be dead," Erik croaked.

"I wouldn't recommend a cold enema," my mom said, as if from prior knowledge. Erik and I looked at her and started laughing. John walked in to see what the discussion was about.

"Perfect," Mom said, handing John the enema bag. "Maybe we can have Seymour Lipps do it."

Though Erik refused the ice-water enema, he recovered. It turned out it was just a sore throat. He was not 100 percent on the flight to

Helsinki but he was good enough to get on the plane. And, on a more promising note, his skin felt suitably desensitized from Trisha's treatment.

Mom was excited that the family vacation had begun. One of her greatest pleasures was to keep a running tab of every family member's likes and dislikes going back thirty years. She remembered that when I was seven, I craved pecan pie for a few months. Now pecan pie was in the "Josh likes" column in her head. Once something was on the list, it was impossible to remove. For her, the world was a vibrant, strobe-lit manifestation of her children's tastes and it allowed her to participate in the world as she thought we saw it.

"Lesbians, Alissa," she whispered as loud as she could. We were on the bus from the Helsinki airport and two short-haired women were standing on a street corner outside the window. I supposed short-haired women were now in the "Alissa likes" column.

Alissa had already seen the women, concluded they weren't lesbian, and testily informed my mom.

"Girls, Erik," Mom deftly rebounded, nodding at the same pair.

It was annoying. But the more annoyed we got, the more Mom tried to get closer to us. It was a spiral into maternal anxiety that played out on the two-hour drive from Helsinki to Heinola. John liked to golf, so she pointed out two plainly visible golf courses, as if he couldn't see them. She drew Alissa's attention to horses and a dog because Alissa once wanted to be a vet. Erik, who collected plush cows when he was eleven, was told to look at the cows in a roadside field. I got boats, a museum, and lakes ("Lakes, Josh"). I wasn't aware that I had a particular affinity for lakes. I think she was getting desperate. It was gut-wrenching to be a part of because she knew we were increasingly ignoring her when the one thing she wanted was to be included. It felt like we were stuck—trapped in our own corners of the car.

"Oh, my god," Mom said slowly as we approached the outskirts of Heinola. "It's a blowhole, Josh."

"Uh-hunh," I said mechanically, trying to focus on a magazine.

"You're not even looking," she said, sounding angry and hurt at the same time. "I guess you've just seen everything already, haven't you?" Her tone was rising. She was starting to sound hysterical in the front seat. "Your mother's just some old lady, is that it? I'm not hip? I'm not cool enough? I don't know anything? Well there's a FUCKING BLOWHOLE IN THE MIDDLE OF FINLAND AND NOBODY'S LOOKING AT IT!"

John slammed on the brakes. The yelling shocked him. We slowed to a crawl on a bridge overlooking the town of Heinola. The car was ringingly silent for a moment as we processed what she had just said. And then we looked back on the left and, rising out of the middle of the lake, there was a fifty-foot column of spurting water shooting into the sky.

We checked into our hotel down the road from the blowhole. The receptionist explained that the town turned on its "lake fountain" during the summer months. Since it was artificial, it was not the same as the Hawaiian, Mexican, or Australian blowholes, but I still viewed it as a good omen. At least this one actually spouted. Right now, that was the only thing we had going for us because Mom was pissed, Alissa was trying to fade into the background, Erik still didn't feel great, and I had eaten so much sea salt that my lips had puckered.

John was the only happy one among us. Finland felt right to him, in part because everyone looked like him. Walking down the street to dinner in Heinola was like flipping through the pages of his family album. One guy we passed looked just like Uncle Denny and a lady across the street could have passed for Cousin Cindy. It was like he'd never left home.

The only problem for him was the language. Most Finns speak perfect English, but John couldn't stop himself from using his own unique pidgin with them. For twenty years, he'd been doing business with a Japanese man whose English was poor. John had adapted by shouting and dropping all articles, like *the* and *a.* Presumably, the technique had worked, as the two continued to do business. But John made the mistake of using it unabashedly with any non-American.

"You have bathroom?" he pronounced loudly and slowly to our waiter, after the guy had greeted us in flawless English.

"Yes, sir, it's right this way," the waiter said, with a light accent.

Later, when we were ordering, John said, "Salmon good? Yes? Okay, me salmon."

"I'm just wondering," I said in a serious way when the waiter left. "Do you think he understands you better when you speak like a moron?"

John thought I was asking a serious question and looked at me for a moment with an unguarded, kind expression before he realized I was mocking him. Then he looked down at his hands and didn't say anything. He looked hurt. Everybody at the table was quiet.

I felt a wave of nausea sweep over me. I was revolted by myself. So what if John sounded funny when he talked? And so what if my mom expressed her affection for us in an annoying way? The emotions were honest. John was trying to make it easier for people to understand him (even though it didn't work) and my mom just wanted us to include her in our lives. And all I could do was make fun of them?

"I thought we weren't going to make fun of each other on this vacation," my mom said.

She was right. I was too mean. At age twenty-nine, I was still acting like a child, not a mature man contemplating fatherhood. I felt like I needed to take a really hot sauna and bake all the anger and sarcasm out of me. Luckily, I had come to just the right place.

The Heinola Summer Theater was a tented space with raked cement seating that could accommodate nearly a thousand people. It was mostly empty now at ten in the morning on the day of the event. There were no walls, so it felt open and breezy. Two hexagonal, gazebo-like saunas sat on either side of the stage. Each had large windows facing the stands. Video cameras aimed through the windows would capture the action inside and pipe it out to a giant twenty-five-foot-tall rock-concert-style screen hanging beside the stage. Windshield wipers on the windows made sure that the audience got an unfogged view.

Inside, the saunas looked elegant and inviting. Cedar benches lined the back three sides of the hexagon and a large sauna stove sat in the middle. A thin metal water pipe snaked its way up and over the oven—this was the *löyly* "inciter." It would pour out a liter of water every thirty seconds once the event began. The sauna temperature gauge read 102 degrees Celsius: 215 degrees Fahrenheit.

Riku Jaro, the event organizer, greeted us at the registration desk beside the stage. He looked like an executioner. Everything he wore was black: black jeans, black boots, black hair. He told me that the dual saunas ensured nonstop sauna action. While a batch of contestants competed in one, the other would be cleaned out for the next heat. He made it sound as if some contestants had been known to explode.

A lady sitting behind the registration desk handed me a packet that broke all seventy-seven male contestants into heats of five or six people. The last two left in the sauna in each heat advanced to the next round. I was due to go in with a Swede, a Lithuanian, two Finns, and a Belarusian.

Unfortunately for me, the Swede was a guy named Anders Mellert, the Swedish national sauna champion. Thirty of his fans were already settling into the front rows and practicing the inspirational sauna songs they'd written for Anders. When one of them heard my name, they stopped singing and broke into whispers. One of them, a tall, sexy blond woman, approached me.

"You are Joshua Davis?" she asked. She was holding the heat breakdowns and made a check mark next to my name when I told her I was. "Do you know that Anders is the greatest? Two months ago, he set the new world record at one hundred degrees Celsius. He lasted sixteen minutes."

She pointed Anders out to me. He was pacing back and forth in front of the stage with a blue-and-yellow Swedish headband on. He wasn't very tall, but he swaggered like a big man and spiked his short bleached-blond hair. He was good-looking—like a Swedish Val Kilmer. If *Top Gun* were a sauna movie, he would have been "Iceman." He was gulping down chilled water and ignoring everyone.

"He was stabbed fifteen times when he was a teenager," the lady continued. "He pulled the knife out of himself and then killed the guy with it. That is how high his pain threshold is."

Great. They'd already started the intimidation tactics.

"You're gonna be fine," Erik said, patting me on the back when I retreated to our seats behind the Swedes. "You don't have to beat him. Just aim for second."

"He'll just have to beat the two Finns, the Belarusian, and the Lithuanian," John said. "That should be easy."

When the first round of contestants came onstage in their bathing suits at one in the afternoon, the audience—which had swelled to five hundred—broke into loud cheers. The first heat contained four Finns and a jittery Japanese guy who looked like he'd gotten lost on the way to the community sauna. Once in the sauna, the Japanese guy calmed down until the water hit the rocks. Then he began blinking a lot and gasping for air.

There was no clock for us to keep track of time—a seriously lunkheaded omission for a time-based contest—but we could count the water blasts. When the sixth one hit we knew they'd been in there for three minutes, and that was too much for the Japanese guy, who ran out of the room. A black-clad sauna wrangler cracked open the door, grabbed him forcefully under the arm, and speed-walked him offstage before he could collapse.

The Finns fell in rapid succession two minutes later, dashing wildly out of the sauna just before the twelfth *löyly* blast. Nobody made it past six minutes.

Erik waited backstage. He was in the fifth heat and was nervously adjusting his skimpy Steamy Niemi underwear. I stayed with him to calm him down. He was taking shallow breaths and mumbling biblical passages to himself.

Another Japanese guy was in Erik's heat. We were told that he was a well-known comedian in Tokyo and was doing this for a TV show. A camera crew followed his every movement. He sidled over to Erik and pulled his shorts up, exposing his ass cheeks. The cameraman moved in closer and the Japanese guy slapped his butt in front of Erik.

" 'The Lord is my shepherd,' " Erik said, turning away with an alarmed look. " 'I shall fear no evil.' "

A large, tented chill-down room dominated the backstage. Inside, there were a half dozen buckets filled with frigid water, some rudimentary showers, and a sturdy Finnish woman with a hose. The sauna wranglers intermittently burst through the backstage curtain to deliver weak-kneed contestants to the woman, who assaulted them with the hose. It was the Scots Hose technique Finnish-style. It seemed like the last thing contestants just sprung from the box would want. The extreme-sauna community obviously reveled in pain.

"I think you should start to drop your temperature," I said to Erik and he disappeared into the tent. I could hear him gasp when he dumped a pail of water on his head. He did it five times and came out with goose bumps.

A big cheer rose up from the crowd on the other side of the wall and the final three men from the fourth heat were dragged rapidly backstage. That was Erik's cue. The six members of his group filed out onto the stage like a Roman sacrifice at the Forum.

I dashed around to the front to join the family. As the contestants walked into the sauna, the giant video monitor captured the nervousness on Erik's face. He was trying to look brave but I could tell from the way he glanced at his fellow contestants that he was worried he was the weakest. He didn't want to be the first one out.

When the door slammed shut, the referees swarmed the windows. They pushed their faces up against the glass and cupped their hands over their eyes so they could see in. If it weren't for the video feed, the audience wouldn't be able to see through the referee blockade.

When the first *löyly* blast hit, the referees started knocking on the windows. They pointed at each contestant and waited for a thumbs-up. If somebody didn't give it, he would be disqualified and removed by a sauna wrangler.

A referee pointed at Erik and rapped on the window. His head was hanging and I could see him trying to cool the air by drawing it through his rolled tongue. The referee rapped harder. Erik looked up and gave a thumbs-up, though the look on his face said, "I'm sitting in a boiling cauldron, so how do you *think* I'm feeling?"

Erik told me later that he had focused on the Old Testament story of Nebuchadnezzar's fiery furnace. In the Book of Daniel, Nebuchadnezzar demanded that the Jews of Babylon worship a golden statue. The high priests Shadrach, Meshach, and Abednego refused, and the king threw them into a furnace stoked seven times hotter than normal. The pit was so hot that it killed the soldiers who threw the rabbis in, but when Nebuchadnezzar looked for the rabbis' dead bodies, he saw four forms walking around in the flames. It was the rabbis and God. When Nebuchadnezzar called to them, the men emerged from the flames without even a burned hair.

Inside his own fiery furnace, Erik smiled. He could feel God's presence with him though I didn't see any ethereal beings floating through the mushroom clouds of *löyly* that rushed up from the oven every thirty seconds. After a few blasts, I could see Erik's smile fade. At the fifth blast—two and a half minutes—an older German man named Lothar started shaking his head. The referees pounded the window. Lothar gave the thumbs-down and erupted toward the doors. The wranglers whisked him away and we showed our support for Erik by screaming encouragements and whistling.

"Praise be to the God of Shadrach, Meshach, and Abednego," Erik mumbled.

He was not the first one out; his God was a mighty God. But I could tell he was having trouble breathing. He was still rolling his tongue but didn't seem to be inhaling or exhaling. He glanced at his competitors. The Japanese guy was grimacing but the two Finns were stone-faced and motionless.

Another *löyly* blast hit. Three minutes. The window-knocking ratcheted up a notch. Erik looked stupefied. Sweat trickled down his face and off his nose. He started rocking back and forth and then launched himself toward the door, crouching as if he were in a trench. With God's help, he had made it three minutes and five seconds. The Finns made it past four minutes and won the heat without God's help, but they were Finns. When it came to saunas, they didn't need a higher power.

After the next group—which wouldn't take more than a few more minutes—I was up. I ran backstage again, stripped down to my Steamy Niemi underwear, and pressed Erik for advice after the fat lady with the hose was done with him.

"That was a whole world of ouch," he said, with a hundred-yard stare. His skin was bright pink.

"What can I do in there to make it easier?" I asked.

"The breathing's hard, but the boiling water on your skin is what kills."

"So what's your advice?"

"Pray."

Anders stumbled out of the chill-down room. He was soaking wet and shivering uncontrollably in blue boxers with yellow polka dots. I needed to start my own cooldown, so I congratulated Erik on not being last and ducked into the tent.

It took a lot of willpower to dump a pail of ice water on my head. But I didn't have much time. Each cheer that I heard meant that I was that much closer to my moment in the hot box. I saw my hands raise the pail and, as if they belonged to someone else, I told them to rotate the bucket. They did and I let out an embarrassing yelp. The lady with the hose looked at me eagerly. "You'll get me soon enough," I gasped.

I took the hose and soaked my arms and legs, which was much easier than the pail-over-head routine. But it was also less effective. Anders walked back in, dumped another bucket on his head, started shivering again, and walked out. The challenge forced me to fill up another one and do a second drenching.

The last cheer floated over the wall and the wranglers told us our time was up. We bunched up by the curtain but had to step aside as the contestants from the previous heat were carried past us like felled gladiators. A stagehand kept the curtain open, and we marched out onto the stage. Flashes of light popped in front of my eyes. The Swedes were chanting Anders's name and then broke off into the repertoire of personalized, inspirational sauna songs they'd crafted.

Anders was nearly hypothermic next to me and could barely understand the referee, who was trying to explain the rules to us in multiple languages. The ref looked really stressed. His eyes were open too wide, he was snapping at us in Finnish, and his face and arms were covered in blotchy red patches of flaking skin. It looked like he spent too much time in the sauna. It crossed my mind that this was yet another sign that I shouldn't be doing this, but Erik appeared to have survived. Plus, I'd already ignored so many warnings, one more wouldn't change anything.

We drew numbers and I got a good position. I was last in, on the closest edge of the bench. That meant that the guys who went in ahead of me had as much as ten seconds in the sauna before I was in. It also gave me the shortest distance to the door, which was comforting.

Anders managed to stand up. He was second to last—right in front of me. We'd be sitting next to each other in the sauna. The wranglers looked to see that we were lined up and then they yanked open the doors. We walked in, but not very fast. Nobody was eager to get in.

When I sat down, I was surprised. It didn't feel that hot. The air smelled pleasantly of cedar and it was certainly one of the nicest saunas I'd ever been in. It was very communal. We were all facing the center, where the oven was, and I looked directly across at an older, bearded Finn. I heard a knocking on the window and saw one of the refs looking at me. I gave him the thumbs-up and even managed a confident grin.

The first *löyly* blast hit. The steam definitely burned—it suddenly felt like I was sunburned. I wanted to grit my teeth and show my pain, but hundreds were watching me. I tried to pretend it didn't hurt and eventually the pain faded.

But then the next *löyly* came and the fading sting from the first *löyly* returned with increased forcefulness. The air became dense and superheated. When I tried to breathe in, I could hear my tongue sizzling as the boiling air swept across it. My lungs rebelled and refused to let the air in. This was much worse than Scots Hose. It felt like knives were being drawn across my shoulders. The sweat rolling down my back felt like blood.

The only prayer I could remember from my childhood was " 'Now I lay me down to sleep. I pray the Lord my soul to keep. And if I die before I wake, I pray the Lord my soul to take.' " That didn't strike the note I was looking for. But when I was ten, my mom's friend Dan came over to teach Erik, Alissa, and me how to meditate. He brought an easel with a sheaf of newsprint and drew a picture of a submarine diving to the ocean floor.

"Meditation is like being in a submarine," he said. "But you get to explore your own mind. When you're good at it, you can travel the whole world without ever leaving home."

Erik thought it was the Devil's work, and Alissa was still sucking her thumb. But I liked submarines a lot and took it up. It made me feel calm—a feeling that I was craving desperately right now, so I started repeating my mantra: an ancient Sanskrit word that Dan had given me after hitting a gong.

I stared at the water dripping out from underneath the sauna oven and lulled myself into a trance. But when the next *löyly* volcano whirled up and over my shoulders, the mantra faded to a tiny little voice inside my head, and a much louder, angry-man voice began hoarsely screaming, "Ahhhhhhhhh! Ahhh! Ahh! Ahhhhhhh!"

The voice bulldozed everything out of my mind. All the silly annoyance I'd built up with my mom crisped and crackled away along with sections of my lungs. Why waste time being upset when I felt like I was dying? Why did I ever waste the time—what good did it achieve? This sauna was simmering me into a reduction of myself; all nonessential emotions were evaporating.

"Ahhhh!" The goddamn *löyly* hit again. With the lack of oxygen, my vision began to contract and my thinking clouded. I was anxious for more revelations and wanted to stay until everything was revealed to me in a giant burst of *löyly*. But the edges of the sauna appeared black even though I knew they were brightly lit. I had to turn my head a little to see Anders sitting on my left. He jerked forward and fidgeted with his hands. He was having trouble, too, but nobody was budging. I had lost track of the *löylies* so I didn't know how long I'd been in. It felt like a very long time.

Sanskrit submarine bubble. What was it I was thinking about a second ago? Left ear devil dagger. Oh, my god. This was a nasty way to die. Why was I in here? Who were these sweating men? Were we someone's lunch and they were parboiling us first?

The next *löyly* brought another rush of clarity. I belatedly realized that this was really a very stupid thing to be doing. The pain now felt like a dozen X-Acto knives were racing one another across my back. "I'm suffering, and for no reason," I mumbled.

The solution was beautifully simple. Leave. Get the hell out. It made a lot more sense than staying in. And, as the next *löyly* ripped into me, I could feel the scream that was resounding in my head start to push its way up my throat. If I didn't get out right this second, I was going to start yelling very loudly and the wranglers would have to carry me out.

I stood up and started to move but the pain was overwhelming and I started to black out. I felt trapped because the more I moved, the more boiling air ran across my already scorched shoulders. Even though it was only five feet to the door, that was five feet of exponentially more agony. But my body took over and my legs, which were in the cooler lower half of the sauna, propelled me out as I felt the darkness pushing in on all sides of my vision.

The sauna door flew open and I catapulted forward, landing in the arms of a wrangler. The pain didn't stop. Tears welled up, mixed with my sweat, and dribbled off my nose while the audience cheered and clapped. It was overwhelming. I'd just spent what felt like an eternity in a small, quiet torture chamber and now I was being paraded in front of hundreds of people.

The wrangler dragged me away quickly, limiting my exposure to the crowd. I couldn't even make out the wrangler's face but I was happy he was there. I trusted him. He had saved me, from both the sauna and the crowd. He was looking out for my best interests when I was too weak to do it myself.

My feelings about him changed when he deposited me in front of the hose woman in the chill-down room. I tried to speak but couldn't. My throat was singed. The wrangler disappeared. I wanted to call him a Judas—I could feel the words start to bubble up but the water hit me before they came out.

I suffered first-degree burns over most of my torso. My skin looked like a waffle iron had been repeatedly pressed against it. Pink and red patterns covered my arms and back and I was having trouble moving. Others had it worse. One man's forehead peeled off and another lost the skin on his ears. The peeling skin was dark—like overcooked meat—and bubbled off their bodies.

My time was reported as 3:01. I lasted through six *löylies*, just like Erik, but he beat me by four cheap seconds. Now, after the fact, I was sure I could have lasted another four seconds, though I knew I couldn't have made it to the next round. Anders and the Belarusian made the cut by lasting a little over five minutes.

Mom coated me with a thick, sludgelike layer of aloe vera gel. She thought I should go to the hospital but my head felt as clear as it had ever been. It was only my skin that stung. John was up next, so she forgot about me and tried to convince him that he shouldn't go in.

As the gel dried, I felt like I'd been dipped in Magic Shell and soon wouldn't be able to move. I was still in the Steamy Niemi underwear and was holding my arms away from my sides. I looked like a cartoon kid that permanently froze up after seeing a ghost.

"Are you okay?" asked a young Finnish competitor. He had a giant, jutting blond goatee and Japanese lettering tattooed on his chest. "You look not okay."

If it wasn't for the faltering English and thick Finnish accent, he could have passed for a stoned southern Californian surfer. "I am Markku Mustonen," he said, sticking out his hand.

I forced my arm forward and felt the aloe gel crackle uncomfortably across my body. Markku shook my hand enthusiastically and congratulated me on my sauna-ing. He told me that he placed third last year and really wanted to go all the way this year but it was an unforgiving sport. When I asked him his secret, he explained that he worked at a steel-manufacturing factory. He was the guy who poured the steel and was accustomed to temperatures above 120 degrees. "I like the heat," he said. Plus, he took a Tylenol before each contest.

John and Alissa were soon decimated. John ran out after 2:40, barely edging out Alissa, who only made it to 2:36. We were all dumbfounded by guys like Markku, who only broke a sweat after five minutes.

"It is not so bad until ten minutes," Markku said. "Then it is hell."

He said he'd lasted twelve minutes last year and lost most of the skin on his face, which was maybe why he looked so young and fresh at age thirty-two. His new facial skin seemed baby-soft. "I love sauna very much," he said. "I have four saunas in my home. You must come and see my saunas. I will make sauna for you. I would be very honored."

"How hot are your saunas?" I asked cautiously.

"It is up to you," he responded. "I will make it as you like. Or, if you like it very hot and your mother likes it very cold, she can be in one sauna and you can be in the other. That is why it is so nice to have four saunas."

I talked it over with the family and we agreed to visit him when we drove back down to Helsinki. Markku was endearingly excited to have met us. "It is very good to have a big sauna family."

To seal our newfound friendship, we agreed to make Markku an honorary member of the Steamy Niemis. And since we were all out of the running, we cheered wildly for Markku now. He didn't disappoint, making his advance to the championship round look easy. But for the final six competitors it looked like Nebuchadnezzar's fiery furnace would be too cool. There was pretty-boy Timo Kaukonen, who looked like a smug serial killer with flowing blond locks. He won the championship last year and had returned with a big-league Finnish beer-company sponsorship and an entourage. His archrival, Leo Pusa, placed second last year but was a three-time champion. He was an older man with a look that said he was unimpressed— unimpressed with Timo's blond hair, unimpressed with the size of the crowd, and definitely unimpressed with the sauna. Of the six finalists, none were foreigners—the championship round featured only sauna-hardened Finns.

During last year's final round, the sauna inexplicably cooled down to 200 degrees, and Kaukonen had to sit there for more than sixteen minutes to outlast Pusa. The organizers didn't want the contestants to sweat for too long—it could lead to extreme dehydration. They'd rather scald your skin off—they figured it would grow back. So this year, they had turned the temperature up to 240 degrees and it had a deleterious effect on the contestants. One guy started shaking uncontrollably at three minutes. Huge arcs of clear snot dangled down from his nose. At 3:58, he ducked out. The next guy split at 7:30.

Markku was left in with the heavyweights. There was Kaukonen, Pusa, and a bearded, unsmiling older man named Ahti Merivirta. Merivirta was one of the locals who started the contest five years ago by constantly turning up the temperature in Heinola's public sauna. City officials finally got sick of him messing with the gauge so they barred him from fiddling with the thermostat and formed a once-a-year championship to give his heat-seeking an outlet. Markku told me that nerve endings die as you get older (particularly if you subject them to this type of abuse), and Merivirta's mottled skin looked like a testament to that theory.

Markku was the youngest of the finalists, and I think it messed with his head. Each heat was like a game of poker. Contestants had to decide if they could outlast their fellow sauna-nauts. In the earlier rounds, as soon as the third man bolted, the last two would sprint out immediately. They didn't have to prove how long they could really last. They may well have been only a few seconds away from breaking, but if they could keep a straight face and project strength, they might convince the others that they could stay in for many minutes more.

Markku had gotten it into his head that his skin was more sensitive than that of the older guys and that undermined his ability to stick it out for just a little longer. He buckled at 9:05, one place away from a second bronze medal. It would have only taken him a minute more. Merivirta walked out at 10:15.

It was now a repeat of last year, with Pusa and Kaukonen trying to outsit each other. Kaukonen's entourage began rhythmically chanting his name: "Tee-mo Cow-ko-nin, Teemo Cowkonin!" But it was not enough. Pretty boy called it quits at 11:41 and Pusa sat in for a few more seconds, as if he were still unimpressed with 240-degree heat.

"Next year I will win," Markku told us right after he got out. His skin was purple and venous. "Anyway, it will take that long for my skin to heal."

The Steamy Niemis did not excel in the sauna. The event will not be an advertising boon for Lewis and Clark Sea Salt, but John seemed to be taking it okay. After all, the donation of a pound of salt only cost him five cents.

But as we posed for some final photographs beside the Heinola blowhole, it felt good to be here. The clearness of my thinking persisted along with the burns. I felt buoyant, like I was filled with helium. It seemed to me that I'd sweated out all the heavy, negative energy and that someone would need to tie me down or I'd float away.

The best part was that I wasn't annoyed at my mom anymore. On the way to Markku's house, she insisted we make a detour to breathe the air on a particular ridge. According to her guidebook, the air along this ridge was the purest in the world. Before the sauna contest, all of us kids would have mocked her, mocked the guidebook, and refused to get out of the car. Now we all bounded out and breathed deep. Of course, the site was so famous that the parking lot was filled with cars and we all got a lungful of exhaust.

But even that didn't dampen our spirits. We arrived at Markku's farm and it was like a family reunion. He introduced us to his wife, Tiina, and then showed us the next most important thing in his life: his four saunas. He had a small electric one inside his main house and another three scattered across his five acres of land. The main one was almost as big as his house. It had two rooms, a porch, and its own stream to swim in. Markku already had it heated up and insisted that we get in while he and Tiina prepared dinner.

"Please enjoy," he said, laying out towels, water, and a six-pack of beer. He then darted into one of the sauna's rooms and came out with a guest book. "Please take a sauna and write down your think-

John Niemi

ing. I have just built it myself and want to know how it feels to you. I think it is a very, very good sauna. Maybe the best, but I like to know what you think."

We were left alone to evaluate the sauna. Everyone except Alissa stripped naked. She couldn't fathom how we could actually get back in. She contented herself by drawing pictures in her journal of the dream home she hoped to have someday with her girlfriend. She had shed what Erik referred to as her "angry lesbian mood" and was now just a happy, contented person sitting on a sauna porch in eastern Finland.

The rest of us cooked ourselves and took a swim in Markku's stream. The water was cool and barely moving.

IPSKI-PIPSKI
LIVES

A few months ago, Tara and I moved again, this time to a flat across town. It wasn't any bigger than our last place, but, for the first time, I fulfilled all her ultimatums. It had light, a dining room, *and* a bathtub. I felt like I had crossed the demarcation line into adulthood. To celebrate, I proposed that we buy a turkey baster and get my sperm out of deep freeze in Berkeley. Tara grabbed my crotch, kissed me hard, and told me that last she checked, my testes were up to the task. We could leave the turkey baster out of it.

I'm the first to admit that the past two years of my life have been slightly odd but I told Tara that I planned on being a much more settled person now. I'd shelve my plans to go to India to make a Bollywood movie, back out of the Paris-Dakar off-road rally in January, and forget about moving to Mexico City to start a mariachi band.

Tara squinted her eyes. She tapped her fingers on the new dining room table.

"Okay, we'll all move to Mexico," she said. "You, me, and our baby. I'll play the harmonica."

"They don't have harmonicas in a mariachi band," I said, smiling.

"That," she said, pulling me into the bedroom, "will be the least of our concerns."

In a few days, Veerabadran will don a pair of ill-fitting swim trunks, wade into a municipal pool in Chennai, and begin his quest for the unassisted nonstop floating record. He'll stare up at the sky for days, turning the clouds into images of Mrs. Veerabadran. Bleachers will line the edge of the pool so that his friends and family can watch him float. It makes me happy to think about it. I can already see him bobbing around all by himself in the big pool, observed by dozens of people. In a strange way, Veerabadran has perfected the art of maintaining the thrill in life for himself.

Jeff Thomchesson has had a harder time with that. Poland was not a good experience for him. The food gave him indigestion and he lost in the semifinals. He was no longer a world champion and returned dejectedly to Houston. But Stephanie, his girlfriend, wouldn't let him mope. She insisted he enter the next big Houston tournament. With Stephanie cheering him on, he shook off his depression and beat every challenger to capture first prize, an all-expenses-paid trip to Acapulco. Jeff, who recognizes opportunity when he sees it, got down on one knee onstage, asked Stephanie to marry him, and whisked her away to Mexico for their honeymoon. When he got back, he called to tell me that his forearms looked bigger than ever and he'd never felt better.

A couple of months ago, Maru celebrated his retirement with ten thousand people at a stadium in Tokyo. He invited me to come but I was on assignment for *Wired* in South America. I sent him a copy of a Black Eyed Peas album and invited him to stay with Tara and me if he ever wanted to visit San Francisco. I promised not to make him sleep on the couch like all our other guests. He wouldn't fit on it anyway. We'd just give him the bed.

Markku has invited Tara and me to vacation with him and his

wife on the Yucatán this spring. Tara is a little wary. Markku asked his Finnish travel agent to find him the warmest springtime resort. He was told to go to Cozumel. If he doesn't find the coastal temperature adequate, Markku is likely to insist we rent a Jeep and drive inland until he finds a temperature he likes. Tara thinks we'll get lost in the jungle searching for hot flashes. It sounds interesting to me.

In the meantime, John's got a new business idea. He's trying to sell Amish-style barn raisings to contractors in the Pacific Northwest. He thinks it's the future of home building. He's going to prefabricate the walls and then put the sucker up in one day with a bunch of ropes. I'm praying that it'll work, though I have my doubts. Either way, I told him I'd be happy to help tug on a rope when the time comes.

"Maybe I won't ever pull off something spectacular," John told me recently on the phone, "but that doesn't mean I can't do something normal in a spectacular way."

That just about sums it all up.

I've come to believe that America truly is the land of opportunity, just maybe not the opportunities we expected. Since World War II, we've lived in a broadcast world, where ever larger and more pervasive marketing campaigns have tried to convince us that we all like the same things. Ours is a hit-driven culture. In a world with only a few major national media outlets, there's only room for a few rock stars, sports stars, and celebrities. The result is that we've had a limited number of heroes.

That's changing, both because of technology and because we need it to change. Our burgeoning population has outpaced the opportunities that the mainstream offers us. As people begin to seek new outlets for their curiosity (Google, Amazon, meet-up.org), I think they will discover that their tastes diverge from the mainstream. There is untapped potential out there and it's not in the form of budding basketball players. I'm talking about shuffleboard superstars, genius ostrich jockeys, and bar-stool-racing titans. You could be great at something you never considered. It's waiting out there, just a mouse-click away.

I believe that this will be the era of outlandish sports. As a result, new heroes will pop up everywhere. There will be champion cement-block racers and superman arctic swimmers. The quest for distinction will spread globally, in part because the American can-do attitude has been one of our most successful exports. It's so successful, in fact, that one of the greatest realizations of the you-can-be-anything-you-want-to-be-in-America dream is an Indian: K. Veerabadran. His original motivation to start running backward was to beat an American.

I grew up believing that I could be the best at something. To be honest, I haven't found it yet, but I'm not giving up. Maybe my mariachi band will find an audience. It's possible that *I'm* a genius ostrich jockey. Or maybe my kids will think I'm the best. I'd like to think they will. I've already started working on my Ipski-Pipski stories.

ACKNOWLEDGMENTS

For believing in me, with little or no justification, I'd like to thank my friends: Ben Lutch, Gregory Manuel, Kevin Garrett, Sam Ockman, Eric Poolman, Joey Carrapichano, Dave Wolman, Alan Porter, Sergio and Cristian Sessa, Bill and Priscilla Panzer, Nick Thompson, Erik Jensen, Gil Jackson, Joanna Silber, James and Veronica Honey, Dawson and Pamela Bennett, John Nichols, Francois Kirkland, Obie and Eliza Patten-Ostergaard, Jeannie and Mark Koops-Elson, Christine and Chris Fox-Donahue, Susie Hoffman, Rebecca Nesbitt, Hayden Hirschfeld, Elizabeth Glaze, Bill Goggins, Carlos Roig, Scott Gagner, Chris Maliwatt, Alex Papanastassiou, Ben Decker, and Phin Younge.

For helping me believe in myself when I probably shouldn't have, I'd like to thank: Mark Robinson and *Wired* magazine, Rick Jacobs, Mark Tavani, Bonnie Nadell, Keith Fleer, and Creative Artists Agency, particularly Bryan Geers and Shari Smiley.

For not disowning me (at least, not yet): Janet, John, Erik, and Alissa Niemi, Peter and Danielle Davis, Rebecca Walls, Vida and Elliot Barron, Carole and Truman Foster, Randy and Carriann Hadland, Poornima Nayak, Shamus Roller, and Maya, Larissa, Mark, Sarah, Joanne, and Mohandas Kini.

And last, to my lovely, talented, beautiful, and extremely patient wife, Tara. This book is dedicated to you.

ABOUT THE AUTHOR

Though young, JOSHUA DAVIS has accumulated a lifetime of failures. In grade school, he electrocuted himself while trying to construct a fully operational replica of the USS *Kitty Hawk* in his bathtub. In high school, he started a rock band and at its first and only performance forgot the lyrics of the band's one song; the group disbanded. After college, he directed a feature-length film about a group of friends living in northern California; the movie was bought by a shady distribution company in Nicaragua. The plan: Recoup the investment by showing the indie film on Panamanian buses. The distributor soon declared bankruptcy and never paid for the film, and Davis went to work as a data entry clerk at the phone company.

The Underdog is Joshua's first book. In the course of writing it, he snuck into Iraq to cover the war for *Wired* magazine, for which he is now a contributing editor. He lives in San Francisco with his wife, Tara. More of his writing can be found at www.joshuadavis.net.

ABOUT THE TYPE

This book was set in Trump Mediäval, a typeface designed by Georg Trump for the Weber type foundry, Stuttgart, in 1954. It is a sturdy and distinctive text face, notable for its wedge serifs and angular yet clear letterforms. These characteristics give Trump Mediäval a high level of legibility under a variety of printing conditions.